SOME PRESIDENTS
Wilson to Nixon

BOOKS BY WILLIAM APPLEMAN WILLIAMS

American-Russian Relations, 1781-1947

The Shaping of American Diplomacy, 1763-1955:
Readings and Documents in American Foreign Relations

The Contours of American History

The Tragedy of American Diplomacy

The United States, Cuba and Castro

The Great Evasion:
An Essay on the Contemporary Relevance of Karl Marx
and on the Wisdom of Admitting the Heretic into the
Dialogue About America's Future

The Roots of the Modern American Empire:
A Study of the Growth and Shaping of Social
Consciousness in a Market Place Society

Some Presidents: Wilson to Nixon

Some Presidents

WILSON TO NIXON

by
William Appleman Williams

A NEW YORK REVIEW BOOK

Distributed by Vintage Books
A Division of Random House, Inc.

A NEW YORK REVIEW BOOK
Distributed by Vintage Books,
A Division of Random House, Inc.

Published by The New York Review
250 West 57th Street
New York, New York 10019

Copyright © 1972 by William Appleman Williams

Library of Congress Catalog Card Number:
72-78148

First Printing July 1972
Printed in the USA

Acknowledgment

I offer this collection as a public thank you to Leo Huberman, Paul Sweezy, and Carey McWilliams, generous and helpful editors who first gave me the opportunity to publish such essays; and to Robert Silvers, who kindly reopened that door in later years.

Contents

Introduction   *page* 11

I   Wilson   19

II   What This Country Needs ...   33

III   FDR and His Shadow   51

IV   Officers and Gentlemen   61

V   Ol' Lyndon—and JFK   83

VI   Excelsior!   109

Drawings by David Levine

SOME PRESIDENTS
Wilson to Nixon

Introduction

Essays initially written as separate pieces cannot be collected in a way that wholly satisfies either the author or the reader. The writer wants to rework them at his leisure in order to develop certain themes in a coherent and sustained fashion, and to compensate for various weaknesses that inevitably appear when one is laboring under restrictions on time and space. The reader wants the same kind of revision. He is laying his money, his time, and his mind on the line, and he has a legitimate claim to a fair return on his investment.

I have done two things to soften the frustration created by the publication of articles that have not been integrated into what I consider—as a reader as well as a writer—to be a full-fledged book.

First: I have made some changes that, within the limits of the form (and the publishing schedule), I hope will clarify certain points, and have expanded my thoughts on various matters that are related to an evaluation of the men—and the office—discussed in these commentaries. I have not knowingly changed the initial character of any specific essay. The books I considered in the original essays are listed at the opening of each chapter.

Second: I have tried, in the following brief remarks, to outline the major themes that I would use, under ideal circumstances, to expand these reviews into a book. I ask the reader to respond in a spirit of understanding that will enable him to develop his own thoughts on some vital issues. The purpose of a book, after all, is not to con the reader into like-mindedness, but to initiate a dialogue about our common condition.

Which at this point is not at all good.

So, first of all, the Presidency per se. To get right down on it, it is a hell of a job. The reality of it often reminds me of the famous line that Thomas Hobbes wrote to describe existence in England during the early seventeenth century: "the life of man [is] solitary, poor, nasty, brutish, and short." That most Presidents stay sane, let alone that a very few of them have done so well, is cause for awe. By comparison, managing a corporation is doodling in the sand at Acapulco—or projecting reality out of your id. Fun, but irrelevant.

The essential problem of the Presidency is defined by these elementary factors: the size of the country and the market place politics that emerged during the breakdown of the upper-class leadership imposed by the Founding Fathers. There are only two ways to govern a continent. One is to assert and enforce the will of a minority or a well-organized plurality. The other is to divide the continent into natural regional communities and allow each people to decide its own fate—including its relationships with other such communities.

In order to impose its will upon a population suckled on the Rights of Free Englishmen, any minority must rely on its own morality, its own intelligence and ability to devise effective programs, and on the arts of persuasion. The upper-class leadership that seized power in 1786-1787 (the Founding Fathers) fulfilled those requirements rather impressively for a generation. Led by Presidents that understood the problems of state-building, they created a functioning political economy, asserted the integrity of that system against the opposition of more advanced European powers, developed a mind-boggling ten-year program of internal improvements designed to integrate half a continent into a conservative community of sorts, stopped the slave trade, and even discussed seriously the morality, the wisdom, and the expediency of ending slavery.

The trouble was that they did not build a social movement committed to those objectives. A social movement is not an elite that overawes or manipulates the population. A social movement is not an interest or a pressure group—not even a large one. A social movement is a strong plurality (on the verge of becoming a majority) of citizens united by common values and committed to action to realize and honor those values. Building and maintaining a social movement is nitty-gritty work, intellectually as well as politically, because it involves creating a consciousness of purpose that resolves conflicts of interest by developing a common interest rather than by arranging temporary bargains in the market place.

If the Founding Fathers had been willing to settle for half a continent (and, ideally, even less), they might have built a social movement based on their upper-class values, and then have gone on to create a possibly exceptional variation on the classic kind of conservative and stratified community. That approach would have allowed Aaron Burr and others to have pursued their different visions of community with sufficient resources. Even the Indians and the blacks could have had a meaningful choice. But the Founding Fathers were in the end not willing to make that hard decision (though they did discuss division into regional governments), and so neither was anyone else.

Once Americans started west without a commitment to the principle that the continent would be developed by multiple (if interrelated) commonwealths, there was no end to the expansion of one empire until they confronted themselves in Cuba and Vietnam. The issue was raised, of course, by the Southerners who asserted and acted upon their right to maintain a stratified community of whites living off the labor of black slaves; but the question of the right to go to hell in one's own way was fudged by white Northerners who answered it by setting limits on that right. That is, by white Northerners asserting—and enforcing with guns—the proposition that Southerners (black and white) must go to hell in the Northern way because it offered more freedom. That maxim contained a measure of truth, though we now know how limited it was, but the crucial point is that ending chattel slavery in that fashion played a major part in sustaining the momentum of imperial expansion. It seems to me impossible not to wonder, seriously, if all of us—black and brown and red, as well as white—would not be further on down the road toward realizing our common humanity if the North had allowed the South to go its own way, thereby forcing everyone to come to terms with the race issue in a far more frontal manner.

But that did not happen and hence the dynamism of imperial expansion increasingly defined the development and the nature of the Presidency. To defeat the Confederacy, for example, Abraham Lincoln vastly extended the implied powers of the Executive and strengthened the practice of intimidating or by-passing the Congress and the courts. Such specifics dramatize the central factor in the process: without a social movement based upon the recognition of limits, and upon the values that define a democratic community, there is no politics except special interest politics in an imperial market place political economy.

Such groups have upon occasion involved a plurality, even a majority, of the population; but special interest groups in a market place society are inherently limited by the underlying ethic of competitive individualism. They cannot create a community. They are at best reformist within a capitalistic framework. And at worst they become involved in extending the market place *Weltanschauung* into other areas and over other peoples. That transforms them into expansionist movements.

The only social movement of the twentieth century developed under the leadership of socialist Eugene V. Debs. It sought to unite Americans of many different interest groups in a common effort to reorganize capitalist industrial society as a democratic community. Debs generated growing support after 1900, and the socialist movement became an increasingly important voice in the dialogue about the future of America, and elected significant numbers of its spokesmen to public office.

That success exerted a powerful influence on the concurrent effort by a small group of capitalist leaders to impose a corporate system on the market place which had come to be dominated by the large corporations. Their strategy was to construct a façade of community based on the false syllogism that capital and labor shared a common interest, and then, behind that piety, to take actions that would preserve their power and sustain a political economy in which the members of the tiny upper class were the only remaining capitalists.

The Presidency rapidly became a crucial factor in a two-front struggle to block the socialist challenge and simultaneously maintain the corporate system. The reason for this was that most corporation leaders lacked any sense of the Tory tradition of *noblesse oblige* that might have enabled them to establish the basis for a conservative yet responsible social movement that could attract the support of middle- and lower-class citizens. The few who did understand the problem confronted the extremely difficult task of devising a workable corporate system, and then educating and persuading their less imaginative associates to accept such a strategy for survival. As those men initiated that effort during the 1890s, moreover, the more perceptive among them realized that the Presidency was central in their strategy in a way that transcended the traditional importance of the office in market place politics. For if a corporate *system* were to be created, then the President was the only available chairman of the board.

Mark Hanna had a better sense of that truth than most other members of the corporate elite, and he saw William McKinley as the man best able to begin the process of traditional importance of the office in market place poliably correct (especially if one emphasizes the vital point of getting elected), and McKinley was moving in that direction when he was gunned down by an anarchist in 1901 as he began his second term. That was an assassination that clearly dramatized and accelerated a change that otherwise would have taken much longer—and might even have been turned in another direction. For Theodore Roosevelt did grasp the problem and he also understood the rudiments of the Tory tradition. His political strategy was simple: use the existing reformist movements to begin constructing a corporate system while at the same time re-educating them in the new outlook, and use the power of the Presidency to cajole and persuade the reluctant members of the upper class. The President thus became a vigorous activist in two crucial areas: initiating and controlling measures that were needed to reform and rationalize the political economy, and guiding the thinking of the citizenry.

Roosevelt also understood the necessity to expand the American economy into the world market place, and was wholly confident that such imperialism would extend the freedom, prosperity, and welfare of all concerned. He relished his enlargement of Presidential initiative and power in foreign affairs. And he slowly came to realize that the corporate political economy could not function without intimate and extensive collaboration between corporation leaders and the President, or without subsidies supplied by the taxpayer. The latter point was not fully comprehended, or institutionalized, until the Great Depression of the 1930s, but the learning process began under the first Roosevelt.

The President thus became the key figure in the effort to construct a corporate system that would function effectively, and thereby undercut the appeal of alternate proposals. The inherent difficulties of building such a political economy, coupled with the emergence of criticism at home and the demonstrated viability of other approaches throughout the world, further centralized power in the Executive. The idea and the ideal of creating a corporate social movement were increasingly lost in the struggle to maintain the existing system in the face of domestic failures, and against the growing challenge posed by radical alternatives to capitalism.

In that process, leadership steadily degenerated into manipulation. Dialogue was subverted by secrecy and evasion. Trust was undermined by lies. And the residue of confidence was further eroded by incompetence and failure.

The Presidency is thus in crisis because the system is in crisis. The only way to resolve the crisis is to build a social movement capable of creating a federation of democratic communities. That means, as a beginning, the assertion of public power against Presidential power. And that involves electoral power exercised at *all* levels, followed by sustained agitation and pressure on those elected representatives. That effort can extend and intensify the kind of dialogue that is essential to building a movement with the ideals, ideas, and credibility necessary to realize our potential as human beings.

It is not an easy life. It is not a short-term or an occasional life. But it is the only life that can improve our present unhappy existence. Radical reforms, let alone revolutionary changes, are wholly dependent upon the creation of a social movement determined to create American communities. That is the only life worth living: indeed, it is the only way to live. To give, that is, each in our own way, to each other.

As someone once said, a loving marriage is predicated upon each person going 75 percent of the way.

Meaning that a revolutionary social movement determined to create a community is a loving marriage or it is nothing.

We *are*, after all, *all* of us, in this together.

[18]

I

Wilson

The growing awareness that the interventions in Cuba, Santo Domingo, and Vietnam were not accidents, mistakes, blunders, or aberrations has not produced much serious discussion of the process whereby such action became the American Way of dealing with the restless natives of the empire. It is not enough to say that the United States has been sending the Marines ever since Thomas Jefferson dispatched them to North Africa in 1801 to clear the way for American commerce. Or to reiterate that the price of freedom is eternal intervention. The issue involves two complex and interrelated developments. One is the gradual confluence of various economic, ideological, and political arguments for expansion into an integrated and dynamic theory of empire. The other is the gathering of psychological momentum behind the propensity to use force in dealing with challenges that appear

Woodrow Wilson's China Policy, 1913-1917 by Tien-yi Li (Octagon)

The Higher Realism of Woodrow Wilson and Other Essays by Arthur S. Link (Vanderbilt University Press).

The Papers of Woodrow Wilson, Volumes V-XI, edited by Arthur S. Link and Associates (Princeton University Press).

Joe Tumulty and the Wilson Era by J. M. Blum (Archon Books).

Revolution and Intervention: The Diplomacy of Taft and Wilson with Mexico, 1910-1917 by P. E. Haley (MIT).

to threaten the integrity of the empire.

Neither of those elements can be fully understood until the Cold War is decapitalized and viewed as a confrontation that occurs throughout our history instead of one that began in 1944 or 1945. It is helpful, but not helpful enough, to push the date back to 1917, when Thomas Woodrow Wilson squared off against Lenin. Wilson played a major role in integrating all aspects of American imperial expansion, but his first major clashes came with the Chinese in 1913 and the Mexican revolutionaries—not the Bolsheviks. His response to the Kuomintang's rising against the Chinese president and militarist Yüan Shih-kai and his sustained meddling and intervention in Mexico tell us a great deal about the true nature of the cold war, though we have been slow to comprehend the evidence.

Professor Tien-yi Li's book on Wilson's China policy shows that Wilson backed Yüan in spite of his undemocratic rule because he wanted a China able and willing to function within the framework of the Open Door Policy. The Kuomintang appeared as a threat to what Wilson had earlier defined as America's duty to open and transform China by imposing "the standards of the West."[1] As for the Mexicans, they were mounting a noncommunist revolution that said no to orthodox Western capitalism, no to Western (and particularly Anglo-Saxon) parliamentary politics, and no to Western individualism.

Those revolutions help us to realize that the cold war actually began with the triumph of laissez-faire capitalism

---

[1] Wilson, "Democracy and Efficiency," *Atlantic Monthly* (1901), p. 292.

over the more organic political economy of mercantilism, and can be dated by the publication of Adam Smith's *Wealth of Nations* in 1776. So defined, the cold war is a major historical phenomenon to be understood as an ongoing confrontation between modern Western capitalism and its domestic and international critics. The antagonism has been visceral and persistent, has involved organic conservatives as well as socialist and communist radicals, and has often flared into violence. The main reason we have mistaken the postwar duels with Russia and China for the real cold war is that they were the first large nations to be successfully organized by the critics of capitalism.

Viewed from this perspective, Wilson emerges as a pivotal figure in the counterattack mounted by Western capitalism. He realized that capitalism had to devise a strategy that would meet the devastating criticism of the individualistic nineteenth-century market place society that was already current when he was a professor at Princeton, and at the same time sustain the imperial expansion of the West throughout the world. All the books discussed in this chapter contribute to our comprehension of how he approached the problem, of his role in creating a spell of psychological urgency to meet and master the challenge, and of his program for victory.

The long debate about Wilson's shift from the individualistic, anti-trust, competitive market place approach of his New Freedom campaign of 1912 to the corporate outlook of the New Nationalism during and after the campaign of 1916 offers a classic example of how historians can recognize a crucial part of the story and then lose the issue by isolating it outside the pattern of long-term development. Thus Professor Arthur S. Link, in his book

The Higher Realism of Woodrow Wilson, concludes that political expediency explains the change: Wilson compromised his true views—the views that led him to create the Federal Trade Commission and to sponsor more than ninety anti-trust prosecutions—to win re-election in 1916. Professor Melvin I. Urofsky in his book on Wilson and big steel agrees that politics was a contributing factor, but prefers to emphasize the pressure on Wilson to abandon "irrelevant" ideas when faced with the responsibility of dealing with the existing corporate system and the necessity of working with the corporations after the outbreak of World War I.[2]

As a few other scholars have seen, Wilson's own writings suggest a different interpretation. The key to the contrast in interpretation involves the nature of Calvinism, and Wilson's reading of that philosophy. Link views Wilson as "a Calvinist and a Presbyterian"; indeed, "the prime embodiment, the apogee, of Calvinistic tradition among all statesmen of the modern epoch" (a rather casual judgment from one who lived through the years of John Foster Dulles).[3] But I think Link is wrong in viewing Calvinism per se, as well as Wilson's understanding of Calvinism, as leading to an individualistic outlook. Calvin was corporate to the core, and Wilson himself recognized that (no doubt with assistance from Edmund Burke) long before Link dates the transformation. Link acknowledges that Wilson began to abandon intense individualism some-

---

[2]Urofsky, *Big Steel and the Wilson Administration: A Study in Business-Government Relations* (Ohio State University Press, 1969), pp. xi-xii.

[3]Link, *The Higher Realism*, p. 4.

time about 1906-1909, but that admission seriously undercuts his argument that the political necessities of the campaign of 1916 explain the change.[4]

The point is underscored when we read Wilson in the volumes of his papers, which Link has been editing over the years. Wilson writes in 1885 that "homogenity of race and community of thought and purpose" are essential: vital to acting "as an organic body."[5] That not only echoes Calvin but sounds very much like Richard T. Ely, the Johns Hopkins economist and advocate of "Christian socialism" with whom Wilson was studying during those years.[6] Even Link admits that Wilson's *The State* (1889) contains "a heavy attack against individualism, laissez faire, and Social Darwinism." "Above all," Wilson insists, "order is absolutely indispensable to progress of any sort." Keenly aware of the crisis confronting America at the end of the nineteenth century, he still omits from his contemporary essays any mention of Coxey's Army, the group of jobless men who marched on Washington following the Panic of 1893, or of the Pullman Strike in 1894, which resulted in the jailing of Eugene V. Debs.[7]

Instead, he tells us that "properly organized democracy is the best government of the few. This is the meaning of representative government." Spinning along that line of logic toward the Pentagon Papers, he adds that "no democracy can live without a leisured class capable of

---

[4]Ibid., pp. 17, 31.

[5]Wilson, *Papers*, vol. V, pp. 74-75.

[6]Link, *The Higher Realism*, p. 38.

[7]Ibid., p. 30; Wilson, *Papers*, vol. IX, throughout the years 1894-1896; vol. X, pp. 102-119, 295; vol. XI, pp. 97-99.

thinking on the problems of government." Thus the most capable and responsible among us (including Thomas Woodrow Wilson, of course) "must find or make, somewhere in our system, a group of men to lead." Not least among the problems to be dealt with arises from the unhappy fact that democracy is "sometimes mistaken for a basis for socialism." The true and good leader realizes, of course, that "political democracy is one thing, *economic* democracy another." The need for strong and wise guidance from above is apparent: "Revolutions always put things back, and sensible reforms are postponed."[8]

So we return to the problem of Wilson's rhetorical switch during the campaign of 1916. I would suggest that Link is correct if we move his judgment involving expediency back to the year 1912. That gives us a Wilson understandably nervous about moving from New Jersey to the national arena, influenced by the intellectual and psychic pressure from Louis D. Brandeis, and therefore by Brandeis's views on the virtues of economic competition, and shrewd-as-hell in his own right as a politician who very badly wanted to be President. That means he lacked full confidence in his own perceptive analysis of the imperatives of Western capitalism while being confident of his reading of the body politic. Perhaps encouraging moral and sophisticated competition by American business would rejuvenate the political economy; but in any event such encouragement offered the best strategy for winning the race against William Howard Taft and Theodore Roosevelt. Expediency in 1912 rather than in 1916. Or,

---

[8]Wilson, *Papers*, vol. V, pp. 74-75; vol. X, p. 235; vol. IX, pp. 117, 129.

more exactly, domestic expediency in 1912 and foreign policy expediency in 1916.

Wilson's domestic policy does appear to be contradictory and confusing if one approaches it with Link's concept of individualism versus corporate nationalism. For in origin and intent many of the proposals represented an effort by the middle and lower classes to discipline and control the corporate giants that had come to dominate the American political economy. They wanted more equity, and they were struggling to preserve their place, but that did not mean that they were trying to re-create the classic individualistic capitalism proposed by Smith and Americanized by Andrew Jackson. The objective was to re-enfranchise the ordinary citizen in the new system that had been created through the process of competition destroying competition. As for the sophisticated members of the upper class, they likewise sought order and balance and restraint—that was their strategy for preserving their power.

Wilson's essential corporatism enabled him, quite naturally and honestly, to agree with both groups. His goal was an organic, conservative, corporate America in which all constituent elements would be integrated under the leadership of a benevolent elite. His initial opposition to what he called special interest legislation, such as aid for the farmers, flowed routinely from that outlook as further distorted by his limited knowledge of American reality. He was sympathetic in the abstract, but he simply did not initially comprehend either the extent or the nature of the many inequities in the system. When he thought about them at all, Wilson viewed the blacks as a particularly troublesome case of the non-Anglo-Saxons who had to be brought along slowly. But, once the system was put in order, they, too, would improve their naturally lower place.

As for Wilson the diplomatist, Link tells us that he was uninterested in foreign policy and unprepared to conduct foreign affairs. That becomes more than a bit of an exaggeration after one reads Wilson's histories and essays written prior to 1912. Never mind. Wilson learned quickly and soon "acted like a divine right monarch in the conduct of foreign relations." Of course, all that power to push American expansion in keeping with the traditional Open Door Policy was "not for the oppressive exploitation of underdeveloped areas, but for the slow and steady improvement of mankind through the spread of a reformed and socially responsible democratic capitalism."[9] There we have a judgment that is literally correct and yet almost irrelevant. The explanation of that paradox lies in the phrase "oppressive exploitation." For to discuss Wilson's foreign policy around the question of whether or not he was a narrow economic man is to pose a false issue.

Wilson was as much against the "oppressive exploitation" of foreigners as he was against the "oppressive exploitation" of American blacks, reds, and browns. With respect to both cases, however, the point is that he had decided that his way of development was the only permissible way to make progress. Dean G. Acheson was merely paraphrasing Wilson when he offered his explanation of American policy shortly after World War II: "We are willing to help people who believe the way we do, to

[9] Link, *The Higher Realism*, pp. 82, 83, 79.

continue to live the way they want to live." Others could expect pressure to change their ways. Even those many Americans, as Link phrases it, who had to be guided "from provincialism toward world leadership and responsibilities."[10] Thanks to the lessons from Joe Tumulty, Wilson became in his own right a "great stage manager" with a "flair for public relations" and a magic touch in "the use of headlines."[11] Professor Blum's book on Tumulty provides several such insights. Tumulty's activities as a reformer in New Jersey, for example, no doubt influenced Wilson in adopting the New Freedom strategy for the election of 1912; and Tumulty fully understood both the intensity and scope of Wilson's conception of the United States as the elected agent of global peace, proper government, and prosperity.

Wilson was much more, however, than an efficient missionary of proper development. He read Frederick Jackson Turner's frontier thesis to mean that America would find its next frontiers around the globe. He talked about the necessity of market expansion (and the role of government in that process) years before he entered the White House. And he combined those themes in the argument that all peoples must ultimately self-determine themselves in the American Way if America itself was to be secure and prosperous.[12]

---

[10]Ibid., p. 73.

[11]Blum, *Tumulty*, p. 61.

[12]See Wilson, *Papers*, vol. IX, p. 365; vol. X, pp. 574-576; M. J. Sklar, "Woodrow Wilson and the Political Economy of Modern United States Liberalism," *Studies on the Left* (1960), pp. 17-47; and J. Weinstein, *The Corporate Ideal in the Liberal State, 1900-1918* (Beacon Press, 1968).

There were exceptions, of course, as when forces trying to overthrow dictatorships and set up more democratic institutions threatened the stability so vital to American expansion. That was the case, as Professor Tienyi Li notes, when the Kuomintang renewed its rebellion in southern China during 1913. Wilson not only backed Yüan Shih-kai's repression but offered no criticism when the Chinese leader first purged and then dissolved the parliament.[13] As in later years, the larger purposes required intermediate expediencies that were justified by the noble objectives.

And, then as now, some men saw and spoke the dangers of such certainty about the righteousness and necessity of American expansion. Nor were they only or always radicals. The Mexican Revolution posed the problem in visceral terms by challenging American property and investments in the name of self-determination, economic development, and social welfare. Professor P. E. Haley's book on the policies of Taft and Wilson in Mexico has much to teach about American imperial behavior. Taft and his Secretary of State Philander C. Knox were deeply concerned to avoid intervention. They concluded that force would not help the Americans in Mexico, and would probably lead to war.[14] J. Reuben Clark of the State Department, an adviser of considerable insight, summarized the situation with beautiful clarity: "This Government would have on its hands what in reality would be a war of conquest of a people animated by the

---

[13] Li, *Woodrow Wilson's China Policy*, pp. 13, 129.

[14] Haley, *Revolution and Intervention*, p. 31.

most intense hatred for the conquering race."[15]

Powerful special interests generated great pressure for intervention. Professor Clifford Trow has made it clear in a recent article that Wilson resisted that narrow approach.[16] The President's problem, as Haley explains in his illuminating book, was to combine "sympathy for the revolutionaries and their cause and his desire to control Mexico's destiny."[17] Wilson, as usual, pecked it out on his own little portable machine: "When properly directed, there is no people not fitted for self-development"; hence the proper American policy was one of "watching them narrowly and insisting that they shall take help when help is needed."[18] You know who decided when help was needed.

That led to intervention just as surely as pressure from corporations, and it was intervention designed to maintain American economic power in Mexico as part of the broad objective of ensuring "the slow and steady improvement of mankind through the spread of a reformed and socially responsible democratic capitalism." Wilson used the Navy, the Army, and economic measures that denied food to countless Mexicans. In the short run he won, "blocking the consummation of revolutionary reform."[19] And later concessions were never so great as to subvert America's

[15]Ibid., p. 41.

[16]C. W. Trow, "Woodrow Wilson and the Mexican Interventionist Movement of 1919," *Journal of American History* (1971), pp. 46-72.

[17]Haley, *Revolution and Intervention*, p. 7.

[18]Ibid., pp. 137-139.

[19]Ibid., p. 259.

economic expansion in Mexico. It was years before anyone except a few crackpots (on the right as well as the
left) connected saving the world for "a reformed and
socially responsible democratic capitalism" with the de-
terioration of life in these United States.

Yet in another sense the Mexicans were the first
Cubans, the first Russians, even the first Vietnamese.
"With uncommon daring and brilliance," Haley concludes,
"the Mexican revolutionaries refused to tolerate [Wil-
son's] interference."[20] Lenin and the Bolsheviks consoli-
dated and extended their challenge to America's imperial
ambitions. But Wilson had already formulated those ambitions as a coherent body of doctrine and related action.

His Fourteen Points Peace Plan of January 8, 1918,
bluntly presented as "the only possible program," was
designed to reconstruct the international system according
to American principles and thereby make it possible for
the United States to dominate the world political economy without recourse to major wars. Viewed from Wilson's perspective, it was a sound and noble proposal. If he
had not already redefined self-determination to mean self-
determination within the American Way, and under American guidance, he just might have mustered enough support to have created such a system.

A strategy based on honoring the principle of self-
determination, however, would have taken Wilson to
Mexico City and Moscow before he arrived at the Versailles Peace Conference. And that kind of accommoda-
tion might have opened the door to an era of coexistence
that could have made it possible for the United States to

---

[20]Ibid.

have avoided many of its later troubles and terrors. As for what actually happened, Professor N. Gordon Levin, Jr., provides a fine summary in his study *Woodrow Wilson and World Politics*. "The main outlines of recent American foreign policies were shaped decisively by the ideology and international program developed by the Wilson Administration." Wilson sought to ensure the supremacy of the American Way, and that required him to contain the anti-imperialist forces "within the confines either of orderly liberal reform or of legitimitized liberal war."[21]

On his way to the White House, Wilson the historian offered some useful advice on how to read the story. "Look into ancient times as if they were our own times, and into our own times as if they were not our own."[22] If is unfortunate that during subsequent years he seems to have mislaid that note he made in 1885 for a lecture on the study of history. It will be extremely dangerous if we do not act upon his insight and thereby recognize that more of the same outlook will beget more of the same consequences.

---

[21] Levin, *Woodrow Wilson and World Politics: America's Response to War and Revolution* (Oxford University Press, 1970), pp. 1, 7-8.

[22] Wilson, *Papers*, vol. V, p. 20 (September 24, 1885).

II

What This Country Needs...

Herbert Clark Hoover almost never laughed, or so Gene Smith tells us; but I have one of those visions that historians occasionally allow themselves: if one arose very early (sometime during that missing hour 'twixt four and five) and moved very quietly along the upper reaches of the McKenzie River east of Springfield, Oregon, there Hoover would be, just barely visible in the mist—in his waders, standing tit-high in that damnably cold water, a string of trout drifting downstream from his suspender button, one hand with a fly rod and the other with the latest *New York Times Book Review* section, his head and cigar tilted high, roaring at the latest historical account of his failures. His belly laugh would override the rapids because he would already have read a story about voluntary communes in Iowa, Idaho, and Indiana, and another about Julius Lester's beautiful blast at white radicals for having to learn the same thing over and over and over and. . . .

Back in the real world one would naturally assume that old-mod Charlie Michelson[1] killed Olde Herbie dead

---

[1]Michelson was the Democratic Party's publicity agent who mounted a powerful smear campaign against Hoover based on the classic techniques of the false choice and the false syllogism (very similar to the current advertising for Winston cigarettes).

> *The Shattered Dream: Herbert Hoover and the Great Depression* by Gene Smith (William Morrow).

D. Levine 70

between 1929 and 1933. As a kind of live-ammunition training exercise for the subsequent massacre of Alfred Landon.

Not quite. Professor Richard Hofstadter raised him from the grave in a memorable chapter of his fine book *The American Political Tradition*.

But then Professor Schlesinger devoted an entire volume to a counterattack on Hoover as a tune-up job for levitating Godfather Franklin. And Izzy Stone can hardly let an issue escape him without swinging his scimitar at what he assures us is the ghost of Hoover ensconced in the White House as clandestine adviser to Richard Nixon and Billy Graham.[2]

But why?

Why so much labor to exorcise a cold and feeble failure? And why so much reliance on analogy to put down Nixon, a man who has generously stockpiled a public arsenal accessible to all critics?

Smith gives us a clue or two but never uses them. So the place to start is with Julius Lester's wryly devastating comment: "The inability to move beyond a politics of reaction has been detrimental to the growth of a white radical movement." For to discuss Nixon in terms of Hoover, and to define Hoover in terms of the Michelson (and textbook) myths, is to display the mind (and politics) of the knee-jerk. The way to get at Hoover, as well as Nixon, is to pick up on two more of Lester's remarks.

---

[2] A convenient review of the Hoover literature is Murry N. Rothbard, "The Hoover Myth," now reprinted in *For A New America*, edited by James Weinstein and David W. Eakins (Vintage, 1970), pp. 162-79.

The first is his accurate observation that white radicals persistently react to specifics instead of seeing the specifics as part of an integrated system that must be dealt with as a system. The second is his call for "a positive revolutionary program."[3]

Now at this point we must go very slowly because we are so confused (as Harold Cruse pointed out a year ago) that, given a problem, we tend to duck into a cloud of quick-frozen New Deal rhetoric for the solution. Hoover was not a revolutionary. He was not even a modern liberal. And he does not deserve uncritical acclaim. But he was an unusually intelligent, and often perceptive, conservative who understood that the system was a system; that it was based on certain clear and not wholly absurd axioms, and that it would work only if the people acted in ways that honored those principles.

"I want to live in a community that governs itself," Hoover explained very simply, "that neither wishes its responsibilities onto a centralized bureaucracy nor allows a centralized bureaucracy to dictate to that local government."[4] "It is not the function of government," he continued, "to relieve individuals of their responsibilities to their neighbors, or to relieve private institutions of their responsibilities to the public." "You cannot extend the mastery of the government over the daily working life of

---

[3] *Liberation* (June, 1970), pp. 38, 39, 40.

[4] The bulk of the basic information on Hoover, and his ideas and policies, is available in published sources. For ease of reference, most of these quotations have been taken from Ray Lyman Wilbur and Arthur Mastick Hyde, *The Hoover Policies* (Scribner's, 1937). Significant exceptions are noted in the text.

a people," he warned, "without at the same time making it the master of the people's souls and thoughts."

If you are Hoover, that is to say, then your moral imperative demands that you let the system come apart at the seams rather than violate the principles by saving the system *for* the people. One of your principles is that the system is *their* system, and hence the moment *you* save it *for* them you kill the dream. For when you do that you *rule* the people instead of serving the people. And the commitments to honoring principles, and to service, are Quaker creed. Perhaps, even, *the* Quaker faith. And Hoover was a Quaker.

So is Nixon. Of course. So there we have a case of no difference with a fantastic distinction. For Hoover held the dream as if it were the Holy Grail, while Nixon has the Holy Grail carried around in a black box by an aide as if it were the daily code for Armageddon.

Back to Gene Smith and his book. His title is *The Shattered Dream*, yet he shows little if any recognition of Hoover's dream. For Hoover did *not* dream that the system would always function perfectly; or that, in the crisis of the Great Depression, it would right itself automatically and roll on beyond poverty. Hoover's dream was that the people—the farmers, the workers, the businessmen, and the politicians—would pull themselves together *and then join together* to meet their needs and fulfill their potential by honoring the principles of the system.

That dream defined both the basis and the nature of his anti-depression program. In his view, the government could

. . . best serve the community by bringing about cooperation in the large sense between groups. It is the failure of groups to respond to their responsibilities to others that drives government more and more into the lives of the people.

Thus he offered ideas, his own influence, the services of the national government, and increasing monetary help short of massive federal intervention. But he could not go beyond his commitment to the principle that the people were responsible—"this is the people's problem"—and embark upon what he considered the "disastrous course" of centralized, irresponsible, and increasingly irresponsive and manipulatory bureaucracy.

As it happened, he did provide more federal aid than had been offered in any other depression, and would have supplied far more if the Democrats had not defeated or spiked a long list of proposals after their victory in the 1930 Congressional elections. And he did in truth block out the basic shape of the New Deal. But he simply could not give over and admit through his actions that he had abandoned his commitment to an American community and to the spirit and the will of the people.

And that faith had its useful side. Led by Gerard Swope of General Electric, some corporation giants pushed him to endorse a plan, presented as a cure for the Depression, that would have given them official sanction to exercise vast powers over the entire political economy. Hoover erupted in angry opposition. It was "the most gigantic proposal of monopoly ever made in history" and "a cloak for conspiracy against the public interest"—a long step toward fascism. It later became, of course, the blueprint for the NRA of the New Deal.

You have to take Hoover whole. He should have given more direct relief and he should have blocked Swope and his cronies. He should have offered more of himself sooner to the people and he should have held fast to that beautiful faith in the people. The visceral truth of it all is that Hoover was done in by his faith in the dream of a cooperative American community, and by his ruthless intellectual analysis of what would happen if the dream was not honored.

Either the people save their country or it does not get saved. It may get stuck back together. It may get managed well enough to remain operational. It may even get shoved into the next historical epoch. But it does not get saved. Meaning it does not get purified by the people demanding that it operate according to its principles.

Hoover was traumatized by the failure of the people to take charge of their immediate lives and then join together in cooperative action, and by his terrifying insight into what the future would be if the people continued to duck their obligation—or if they settled for less.

Do not laugh. Hoover outlined our future in 1923. We are living in it now. We do not like it. And even yet we have not taken charge of our immediate lives so that we can then come together and create an American community. *We* have *let* the future that Hoover foresaw in 1923 *happen to us*. Hoover *did not do it to us*.

To fully comprehend this, we must understand that Hoover knew modern American industrial society better than *any* other President. It takes one to know one. And he had been one. And had become increasingly disturbed and concerned. Let us begin in 1909, with the chapter on labor in his famous (and still used) exposition of the *Prin-*

ciples of Mining. "The time when the employer could ride roughshod over his labor is disappearing with the doctrine of *'laissez faire,'* on which it was founded." Indeed, unions were "normal and proper antidotes for unlimited capitalistic organization." The good engineer "never begrudges a division with his men of the increased profit arising from increased efficiency." And the good engineer took an honest "friendly interest in the welfare of the men"; and further understood that

> ... inspiration to increase exertion is created less by "driving" than by recognition of individual effort, in larger pay, and by extending justifiable hope of promotion.

Of course it is capitalistic. And of course it has a tinge of paternalism. But it is personal, it is moral, and it reveals an awareness that the past is past—and that the corporation poses a serious danger to community.

The Bolshevik Revolution extended Hoover's awareness of such matters; in part because, as he noted, it "was a specter which wandered into the [Versailles] Peace Conference almost daily," and he dealt with it as an adviser to President Wilson. He naturally opposed communism as being destructive of individuality *and* true cooperation among individuals and groups. But he did understand that the revolution was the work of men and women striving to realize their potential. Misguided as they might be, he acknowledged that they, too, were reaching for the dream.

Even more important, perhaps, Hoover saw and understood the rise of fascism long before most other American leaders. During those same years of the early 1920s, moreover, he extended his awareness of what the corporation was threatening to do to America. The

> . . . congestion of population is producing subnormal conditions of life. The vast repetitive operations are dulling the human mind. . . . The aggregation of great wealth with its power to economic domination presents social and economic ills which we are constantly struggling to remedy.

He then pulled it all together in a perceptive (though horribly mistitled) essay called *American Individualism* that he wrote as he entered upon his long service as Secretary of Commerce (1921-1928). From experience and observation, Hoover concluded that capitalistic industrial society (and specifically America) had become functionally divided into three major units, and that the society was poised on the threshold of becoming a syndicalist system. One group was composed of capitalists, including agricultural entrepreneurs as well as industrial, banking, and commercial operators. The second functional bloc was labor.

The third was defined by a rather tricky concept, that of the public per se. It was in substance, though neither in form nor in rhetoric, a class. That is, it was all the small and middle-sized independents and their dependents—along with labor. Meaning most of us. Hoover was in effect making an analysis of the giants, on the one hand, and the rest of society, on the other: those with national power and those who had to cooperate if they were to avoid manipulation.

> The American people from bitter experience have a rightful fear that great business units might be used

to dominate our industrial life and by illegal and unethical practices destroy equality of opportunity.

From this it followed that two criteria had to be met if the dream was to be fulfilled. First: the government had to act, simultaneously, as umpire of the actions of the three groups *and as leader of the public in coming together in cooperative action*.

Beautiful. And damnably difficult.

It is beautiful because it perfectly describes the dilemma of trying to govern a continent without a social movement that represents the common interest of various special interests, and that is engaged in the process of redefining those separate groups as equal elements of a commonwealth. Honest and intelligent public servants offer the only hope under such circumstances. But Hoover also knew that such government from the top down was difficult because bargains between market place interest groups that were arranged or regulated by the government did not define the true common interest, and because that procedure could so easily slide into manipulation by the government and the strongest interest groups.

Even so, Hoover maneuvered some of it almost beyond belief. As in his successful battle to define broadcasting as a public forum. And as in his use of brain power and moral power to keep wages high in 1929 and 1930.

Compare that with Nixon.

No problem. Nixon has no moral power.

On with Hoover's second imperative: the people had to accept and discharge their responsibility to come together in cooperative action to create "a community that governs itself." Then came the eerie part. The future map. What would happen if the people gave up on the dream? If the corporations took over—fascism. If job-oriented labor leaders took over—a mutant, mundane, and elitist corruption of socialism. If government per se took over—an elitist, bureaucratic, and community-destroying hell-on-earth.

So right it shakes you.

It is easy to say that Hoover's dream involves an unresolvable contradiction: that a people's capitalism of the kind that he envisioned is like a round square. And the criticism is deadly if you see Hoover as nothing more than a Quaker Rockefeller. But when a man talks seriously about the need for grass-roots cooperation in order to secure and maintain the opportunity for individual fulfillment, then he is not discussing orthodox capitalism. He is headed, however cautiously and even unknowingly, toward a transitional kind of political economy. It might indeed be impossible to realize that kind of a society, and certainly we have not created it, but Hoover was correct about the other options if we did not break out of our traditional *Weltanschauung*.

If the people abdicated their responsibility for realizing the dream, and instead relied on the government, Hoover projected a period of increasingly unsuccessful bureaucratic pseudo-socialism. And then, "in the United States the reaction from such chaos will not be more Socialism but will be toward Fascism."

So what we have now is a horrible combination of what he saw as the three possibilities.

But he *must* have failed beyond giving too little relief, beyond waiting too long to give more of himself, and beyond being bullheaded about his dream.

True.

His mishandling of the Bonus Army.

That story is the best thing in Smith's book. He describes it very well, but he does not tell us what it means. To understand that, you have to know the dream. And then face the truth that by 1932 the people had not taken charge of their immediate lives and begun to come together to create a community. Instead, they had begun to petition the government for salvation.

For the feel of how Hoover reacted, do not waste your time ransacking the archives. Just listen to The Doors doing the first verse of "The Soft Parade." His dream was crumbling, dribbling down into Washington by ones and twos. Then by thousands. And he drew the traditional American civilian conclusion. People marching pose a military problem. The explanation for that response is basically simple: the people have done little serious marching except on the way to war.

Now the American military have the patience that begets great power: wait for the civvies to come to us and then we are in charge. And so they were. MacArthur and his minions. The third-person types. MacArthur to an aide: "MacArthur has decided to go into active command in the field."[5]

But the key was Hoover's trauma. That shut him off: confused the desperation of the people with the willful intent of the people. He mistakenly thought they wanted what we have today. So he gave over to MacArthur. And Douglas did his thing. Bayonets, sword-drawn cavalry, tear

---

[5] Smith, *The Shattered Dream*, p. 159.

gas (a baby died), and fire. (And then another failure. For MacArthur usurped power, went beyond his orders, and Hoover did not strike him down.)

But the people only wanted what they thought was the New Frontier—help from the Metropolis for the country. Help from a few of the people for most of the people. In Hoover's view, however, that was impossible. He was correct. The Metropolis is not a few of the people helping the rest of the people. The Metropolis is managers and directors ruling the people. In reality the New Frontier was simply the Metropolis as the center of The Empire, lording it over us at home and abroad with increasing indifference (even contempt) for what Hoover understood as the principles of the system—and for Hoover's dream. If the Metropolis saves the country, it does so by changing what Hoover believed in as the people and the community into The Empire.

Hoover was against The Empire. That was the Quaker. Not Nixon-Quaker. Just Iowa-boy-Hoover-Quaker. Meaning that he Honest-to-God-and-to-the-people simply wanted us to exchange the things we create for the things we need. And to give of ourselves to each other in times of well-being as well as in times of crisis. If we did that, then there would be no government intervention and management in our honest exchange, we would remain masters of our lives, and we would create an American community.

Once again, of course, Hoover can be damned for not breaking free of capitalism. He can be faulted, for example, for not realizing that it was impossible to depoliticize trade and investment in a market place system. But I have the thought that one measures capitalist leaders not by how socialist they are, but by the extent to which they understand and try to overcome the classic inequities of capitalism without at the same time moving toward fascism or bureaucratic statism. As Joan Hoff Wilson convincingly demonstrates in two forthcoming books—a perceptive biography of Hoover and a keen study of the business community and foreign policy—Hoover was willing to work toward a largely self-contained economy, and he was consistently opposed to the assumptions and attitudes that produced the cold war. He told President Harry S Truman in May, 1945, for example, that the United States should be content "to persuade, hold up our banner of what we thought was right and let it go at that."[6] One wonders how many liberals, let alone radicals, would be content with that basic policy; but the crucial point is that the history of the world, and our present condition, would be drastically different if Truman had followed Hoover's advice.

So we come right down on it. The trouble with Hoover was that he believed. Not just in us. But in the very best in us.

To get straight on that is to understand the great strengths of his foreign policy along with his weaknesses during the Depression. The guiding axiom was to act, as a people, in ways that would build an international community. To be a good neighbor. "We have no hates; we wish no further possessions; we harbor no military threats." That meant, *ipso facto*, that he "absolutely dis-

---

[6]Memo on the meeting between Hoover and Truman on May 28, 1945, *Truman Mss.*: Post-Presidential, Individual File. By courtesy of Joan Hoff Wilson.

approved" of the concept of the United States as Big Brother to the world.

Hoover was keenly aware that "a large part of the world had come to believe that they were in the presence of the birth of a new imperial power intent upon dominating the destinies and freedom of other people," and he recognized the necessity for non-imperial—and anti-imperial—action. The Quaker knew it was not enough simply to say that Dollar Diplomacy was "not a part of my conception of international relations."

First things first. Control the bankers. The government, he asserted bluntly, "has certain unavoidable political and moral responsibilities to guide and control such loans." "No nation should allow its citizens to loan money to foreign countries unless this money is to be devoted to productive enterprise." Otherwise the government would be drawn ever deeper into the maelstrom of intervention. That meant no loans to prop up Potemkin-like governments, no loans for military purposes, and none for "political adventure." And it meant no government underwriting because that "placed the risk on the taxpayer and not upon the private banker."

The financiers and their allies were too powerful, and Hoover could not win a clear victory in that battle. He needed help from the people which they never gave. But he blocked the bankers when and as he could, kept the issue before the public, and refused to be drawn into intervention. Thus, when he became President, he promptly published J. Reuben Clark's memorandum on the Monroe Doctrine, a document that President Calvin Coolidge had buried because it destroyed the grounds for using the policy as a sanction for such interventions. Thus he returned to the policy of recognizing Latin American governments without demanding that they satisfy US criteria. And thus he withdrew the Marines from Nicaragua and Haiti, and refused to send them into Panama, Honduras, or Cuba.

Of course, all that principle poses a problem. If you cannot properly intervene for the bankers, neither can you intervene to reform the backward or to block the difficult and the bothersome. Once again the trouble with Hoover was his damn stubbornness about that dream. He was all the time trying to play it straight.

Hoover resolved the dilemma by cutting through to first principles on military policy. The armed forces of the United States had the one purpose of guaranteeing "that no foreign soldier will land on American soil." "To maintain forces less than that strength is to destroy national safety, to maintain greater forces is not only economic injury to our people but a threat against our neighbors and would be a righteous cause for ill will amongst them."

That meant that the Chinese had to meet the Japanese attack of 1931 with their own resources and will. The assault on Manchuria was of course "immoral," but "the United States has never set out to preserve peace among other nations by force"—and Hoover was not about to begin. "These acts do not imperil the freedom of the American people, the economic or moral future of our people. I do not propose ever to sacrifice American life for anything short of this." To intervene in China, moreover, "would excite the suspicions of the whole world." And, finally, a sense of history: "No matter what Japan does in time they will not Japanify China and if they stay long enough they will be absorbed or expelled by the Chinese."

Reminds one of John Quincy Adams. "America goes not abroad in search of monsters to destroy. . . . She might become the dictatress of the world; she would no longer be the ruler of her own spirit."[7]

Herbert Clark and John Quincy: too bad they are gone. Spiro Agnew could spend the rest of his life chasing after them, screaming all the while that it was time to take care of those effete radical-liberal snobs who are undermining and destroying the nation and its rightful place in the world.

So we come back to what the man Julius Lester says: if we concentrate on destroying Hoover, then "ultimately we will destroy ourselves."

What I mean is that Gene Smith tells us that Hoover, in the depths of the hell of 1931, said that "what this country needs is a great poem. Something to lift people out of fear and selfishness."[8]

If you kill a Quaker engineer who came to understand that—and to believe in and to commit himself to that— then you have murdered yourself.

---

[7] 1821 Fourth of July Oration, Washington, D.C.

[8] Smith, *The Shattered Dream*, p. 67.

III

FDR and His Shadow

James MacGregor Burns has a beautiful faith in and commitment to you, the reader. He believes that when you open his book you become Willie Mays and have come to play. There is no sermonizing, no patronizing, and no super-professionalism. Professor Burns is telling us, through a study of Franklin Delano Roosevelt, about our efforts to deal with the two traumatic experiences that shaped the present: the massive social dislocation of the Great Depression and a global war we might have lost. He stays largely in a low key, probably because the tale is so serious, and understanding it so vital. And it is, after all, our responsibility to confront these matters, think about them, and act upon the explicit and implicit meanings and implications.

One gets the feeling, early on, that Burns is warning us to do so or we will be engulfed. The irony is subtle but inescapable: we are reading about successes that barely held the line rather than triumphs that opened the gates to happiness ever after. For he is saying, as I read him, that Franklin Delano Roosevelt was the best in and of us during the frightful years from 1932 to 1946, but that best was simply not good enough. It was not sufficient because, although we won the war, thereby ending the Depression and creating an opportunity to begin to realize

Roosevelt: The Soldier of Freedom by James MacGregor Burns (Harcourt Brace Jovanovich).

our best traditions and ideals, we failed to fashion our politics and our economics in the ways that would enable us to mold a community. And a community offers the only viable technique of survival.

Burns understands that the sole actionable source of community we Americans possessed between 1932 and 1946 was the upper-class, aristocratic tradition of *noblesse oblige*, most strikingly personified by Roosevelt. I say "actionable" for these reasons: Our other traditions of community were neglected, weak, and without intellectual and political leaders who could adapt them to deal with a gigantic and increasingly centralized industrial system. The upper class ruled the political economy; the middle and lower classes very largely looked to that upper class, rather than to their own resources, for leadership. And FDR was the only leader, after Herbert Hoover had failed, who had any real chance to impose the tradition and practice of *noblesse oblige* upon the majority of the upper class—which predominantly held and honored the much narrower outlook of entrepreneurial capitalism as modified by the giant corporation.

From this perspective, Burns—while chronicling the major events between the election of 1940 and Roosevelt's death in 1945—develops two levels of analysis and interpretation, one concerned with individuals and domestic policy, the other with power and leadership in general.

The progression of Roosevelt's physical illness is handled with a rare combination of candor, sympathy, and thoughtful judgment. The President was a courageous man who time and again rallied himself from terrible pain and great fatigue. He lived a racking life, but neither the agreements at Yalta nor the decisions on earlier major events can be explained in terms of an incompetent President.

The anecdotes used by Professor Burns are often extremely powerful. On one page, for instance, we get the bloody juices of those interlocking triangles involving Secretary of State Cordell Hull, Sumner Welles, William Bullitt, and FDR. The President thought Welles "a superb presidential agent" in the morass of the State Department. To Hull, Welles was "the all-American . . . thun of a bitch." Bullitt wanted to take over both roles, and so told stories about Welles making "advances to a Negro porter on a train." Roosevelt knew "that Welles's usefulness was over," but told Bullitt to his face that St. Peter had passed the word: "*You-can-go-down-there.*"

Burns is a kind and sophisticated man with a warm sensibility about dramatic developments in primary personal relationships, and he is exceedingly moving when he describes the increasing distance between Eleanor and Franklin Roosevelt, and the latter's resumption of a relationship with Lucy Mercer Rutherfurd. Burns also penetrates into the heart of Eleanor's importance in goading the President to honor his own—their own—value system.

> Hers was a conscience combined with an almost demonic commitment and tenacity. By now she had come to recognize that she could not have, even if she still wanted, a romantic or even close relation with her husband. . . . They treated each other with devotion, respect, and tolerance . . . and Eleanor had learned to accept her White House role as essentially a presidential aide, though a very special one. . . . But always there was the self-mastery and the passion that led her on to the next column, the next lecture, and the next cause.

Paterson

Eleanor constantly tried to push her husband and his administration into more extensive and effective action to help black Americans achieve equality. Burns is candid about FDR's weakness on this major issue, bluntly observing that Roosevelt "was not a strong civil libertarian"; but, although he recapitulates the high points of that confrontation, he does not explain that quicksand in the vital center, or discuss the terrible consequences of an upper-class leader who saw only white in a world that was mostly colored. And, while his discussion of the erosion of civil liberties—among them, the terrible incarceration of Japanese Americans—is better, Burns, who surely understands the deeper aspects of these and related domestic issues, never explicates Max Lerner's burning insight of 1943: "We shall need to build another bridge of fire, not to link in with our Allies but to unite us with ourselves, and to span the fissure within our own national will."

A similar diffuseness weakens the treatment of Roosevelt and the economy. Whereas Burns is straightforward about the inability of the New Deal to lift the nation out of the Depression, he is much less clear in discussing the very serious limits of President Roosevelt's efforts to deal with the structural problems of the political economy. The President spoke periodically about creating more TVAs, and he offered a striking catalogue of needs and objectives in his January, 1944, State of the Union address, but the dominant characteristic of the Administration was its far more limited concern to keep the existing system operational.

This by no means negligible deficiency affords a touchstone around which Burns explores a broader kind of issue. At the heart of it is the question of leadership and power. Today Roosevelt is routinely invoked by many as the exemplar of all that we need and do not have. Burns will not accept that myth, and therein lies the central importance of his work. Let us consider, as a way of defining the issue, the efforts of the New Deal to overcome the Depression. It is commonly accepted that the war, rather than peacetime policies, pulled the nation out of the Depression. But that analysis only raises several other questions.

There was nothing damning, after all, for a capitalist leader to first try in 1933 to save the system. The crunch came when faith had been rekindled, and the wheels were again in motion. And at that point Roosevelt did not provide sustained leadership on the major issues and problems. The American people, Walter Lippmann realized in 1941, "are not being dealt with seriously, truthfully, responsibly and nobly. They are being dealt with cleverly, indirectly, even condescendingly and nervously." Roosevelt went "down the line," as he remarked in one of his last press conferences, "a little left of center." Although helpful, even crucial in the early years, that stance was not, given the circumstances, either imaginative or bold. The President sensed this, and at one point approached Wendell Willkie about joining forces with him to reorder American politics in terms of liberal and conservative parties. But that was very late in the day, and nothing happened. The legacy of Roosevelt's barely coping, while simultaneously generating a belief in the nation's dynamic successes, is a public unprepared for changes it cannot prevent, ill equipped to choose between alternate ideas and policies, and psychically enfeebled precisely when it needs the internal discipline required for reordering priorities and practicing self-denial.

Moreover, it is easy (and convenient) to forget that the much lamented credibility gap in foreign affairs began with FDR in 1940 and 1941. Burns is masterful in quietly showing how Roosevelt exercised his executive powers to the limit in propelling the nation into an alliance with Great Britain but refused to engage his great abilities and persuasiveness in a continuing dialogue with the public. The issue is not whether Roosevelt allowed Pearl Harbor to happen; it is that, given his unwillingness to confront his critics and the public, there was no other way for the war to start. And it had started in that way in the North Atlantic before the Japanese attacked in the Pacific.

Roosevelt's failure to lead the country into a meaningful and necessary war against fascism, together with his similar pattern in domestic affairs, meant that the nation never defined and dealt with the major issues with candor, realism, and its best ideas and ideals. The result, to begin with, was a narrow application or interpretation of traditional attitudes and policies. Thus the very early appearance of the so-called policy of negotiation from strength, which comes down to an insistence that the opponent accept all the essentials of the American position before peace talks begin. Thus the doctrine of unconditional surrender, a distorted and misapplied "lesson" from the Civil War. Thus the quick birth of the Munich syndrome in dealing with situations that were (and are) not analogous. And thus the meaninglessness of civilian control of the military, because the civilians define the problems in military terms.

At the grandest level of all was Franklin Roosevelt's

projection of the Wilsonian dream of an Open Door world dominated by the United States and Great Britain. A remark by Harry Hopkins, quoted by Burns, catches the essence of the outlook: "The United States, through the espousal of the 'Open Door Policy,' has an absolutely clean record in China over the years. We must keep it so." One does not know whether to laugh or cry—or knock Henry Kissinger's head against the Great Wall.

In concentrating so much on FDR, however, Burns neglects the extent to which the President, given his orthodoxy, was influenced by the men who had been maintaining and applying the Open Door Policy for decades. The author correctly argues that FDR gradually realized the necessity of taking the USSR into some kind of limited partnership. Not only did the early refusal to do so leave Eastern Europe completely open to the politics carried by the Red Army; it also put Roosevelt into the extremely ticklish position that led to the unfulfilled commitment to open a second front in 1943. Burns sees the failure to honor that promise as the major cause of the cold war, and argues that the confrontation was developing before Roosevelt died.

Burns somehow missed the document which makes it clear that Roosevelt was ready, on the eve of his death, to demand that the Russians accept the Open Door Policy or face the coordinated opposition of the Western Metropolis. But he does not flinch in the face of the clear thrust of Roosevelt's policy, which was based on the principle of Anglo-Saxon supremacy. In foreign policy surely, and also very probably in domestic affairs, Franklin Roosevelt represented a convergence of Theodore Roosevelt and Woodrow Wilson. Psychic and bold, intuitive and yet blocked by his fears, he saved America from what he considered the threat of domestic revolution and external fascism at the price of internal statism and the cold war. Thereby the enigma of Franklin Roosevelt. Would a domestic upheaval, or a war against an assault on the Western Hemisphere, have destroyed our identity—or our will to create communities out of a continent? I doubt it. I have the faith that we would have found and realized ourselves.

Be that as it may, the shortcomings of FDR's leadership had equally serious consequences in other, less obvious situations. Neither he nor his administration came to grips with a broad spectrum of issues and problems generated or intensified by the war. It is Burns's effective technique to suggest this myopia while describing the event involved, as in Roosevelt's handling of the atom bomb. But perhaps the point can be made more strongly in connection with an instance of Presidential imagination and leadership. The GI Bill of Rights was a creative piece of legislation; Roosevelt and its other supporters deserve full credit for anticipating and confronting a major problem of postwar readjustment. But there was little or no recognition of similar disruptions, and no sense of the interlocking nature of wartime changes. Thus the GI Bill was a specific solution to one difficulty, yet ignored was the almost certain probability that the pattern of education created by the law would arouse expectations that could not be met without major social and economic innovations. Nor did the Administration consider that such an educational system, with the concomitant wild boom in technology, would operate to stratify the society.

Among other examples, Burns ticks off the government's blindness to the consequences of the serious weakening of the family and the related flight forward of women into the market place; the constant thrust toward trying to solve all problems through greater and more centralized federal power; the revolutionary upsurge in the nonindustrial world, about which there was an almost total lack of understanding. At the outset of his narrative, when he discusses those opposed to intervening in the war, Burns quotes a remark by Charles Lindbergh that haunts the reader as he encounters later issues: "I do not believe we are strong enough to impose our way of life on Europe and on Asia." In the short run, of course, Lindbergh was wide of the mark. He was confused about the nature of the war and mistaken about the power that could be mustered against Hitler. But he had a deep feeling for the truths that America was not powerful enough to control the forces which would be released (and created) by the war, and that the country needed to do much more by way of setting its own house in order.

Because Burns has defined and dealt in this work with vital issues he offers much of significance to contemporary Americans. He makes it wrenchingly clear that the over-forty-five crowd has undergone two social traumas, which make a great deal of their behavior understandable. And understanding *is* the foundation for a dialogue. Burns also reveals how any leadership is constricted without such a dialogue. Most important of all, he has dramatized the need for clear ideas about what to do, and laid bare both the limits and dangers of power without them. Any power. Aristocratic or liberal or revolutionary.

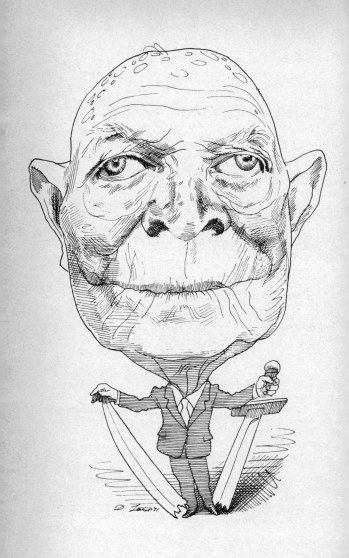

IV

Officers and Gentlemen

You can work through these books (or any others on the military) as many times as you choose, but there remains only one place to begin any discussion—with the two challenges posed by J. Glenn Gray at the end of *The Warriors*.

First the one concerning war itself:

> Nietzsche rightly sees that war-making must be overcome through strength and voluntary decision of a strong nation or group of nations; peace will never

---

The Warriors: Reflections on Men in Battle by J. Glenn Gray (Harper Torchbook).

Military Men by Ward Just (Knopf).

The Years of MacArthur, Volume I: 1880-1941 by D. Clayton James (Houghton Mifflin).

The Papers of Dwight David Eisenhower: The War Years edited by Alfred D. Chandler, Jr. (Johns Hopkins).

Dear General: Eisenhower's Wartime Letters to Marshall edited by Joseph Patrick Hobbs (Johns Hopkins).

The Supreme Commander: The War Years of General Dwight D. Eisenhower by Stephen E. Ambrose (Doubleday).

At Ease: Stories I Tell to Friends by Dwight D. Eisenhower (Doubleday).

Pentagon Capitalism: The Political Economy of War by Seymour Melman (McGraw-Hill).

The Military-Industrial Complex by Sidney Lens (The Pilgrim Press and The National Catholic Reporter).

occur as a consequence of weaknesses, exhaustion, or fear. . . . Prepared for by a gradual change in the disposition of dominant groups, the final stroke will come in consequence of a daring, voluntary, and decisive act of breaking the sword.[1]

If you are ready for that bold move, then your problem is to build a social movement that can effect the required "change in the disposition of dominant groups." Even so, what follows may be of some help to you. For, as Gray points out, "The vast majority of our people want our 'armed peace' no less than their representatives, or, more correctly, they see no alternative to a peace of armed might";[2] and a careful look at the military may help generate among civilians a greater willingness to change their own outlook. That is necessary because the closer one looks at the military the more it becomes apparent that they have truly put their backs into giving us what we said we wanted. First the defeat of Nazi Germany and Imperial Japan, and then victory in the Holy Cold War against Communism. If the second objective now appears implausible or quixotic, even a classic aberration, it is nevertheless our responsibility to change the policy if we want the military to behave differently.

I agree with Gray about the nature of the final blow against war, but I do not think it is very effective to concentrate on that last daring act before we have given new orders to the military. Indeed, we must gather ourselves for that effort as part of changing the outlook of dominant groups. Hence I think it is useful to review our

[1] Gray, *The Warriors*, p. 226.
[2] Ibid., p. 227.

traditions and history so that we can give ourselves over to a confrontation with the immediate issues: 1) how to define and control the force we consider necessary during an interim period, and 2) how to decide when we are justified in using that force.[3]

Those questions immediately involve us with Gray's second challenge: the guilt incurred in doing one's duty when the duty involves inhumane actions, and the more general (or social) guilt one shares as a "participant in a system and an enterprise whose very essence is violence and whose spirit is to win at whatever cost." "If guilt is not experienced deeply enough to cut into us, our future may well be lost."[4]

In view of My Lai, Cambodia, and Laos, that formulation may seem a bit abstract and not focused sharply enough on the specific problems of the military-industrial complex, the bizarre monstrosities and grotesque derangements of the military's effort to accomplish our avowed objective, or the role of the military after Vietnam. If that is so, then I suggest the trouble lies in our growing propensity to abstract our civilian selves from the seat of responsibility and guilt while at the same time we increasingly unload the blame on the shoulders of the military. (Or, the mirror image, to defend the military whatever it does.) The danger in that approach is that it will deepen the pit we have already dug almost to the depth of a grave.

---

[3] I am not dealing with the current literature of exposé because the focus here is on how the military acquired the opportunity for such activities.

[4] Gray, *The Warriors*, pp. 182, 195, 212.

For one thing, as Ward Just explains in his useful book *Military Men*, the military is already working to cover itself on the guilt front. In three ways, that is. First, with its own Vietnam position papers on file in the White House. Second, by punishing some of its own, Lieutenant Calley being the most dramatic case. Third, and most important, with plans for the future. "We are victimized. We are called upon to take abuse from the press and the public for decisions in which we have taken no part. . . . *We want a voice in our own destiny.* We want a reasonable concern that we will be used in a place where it is reasonable to use us, and not improvise policy as we go."[5] That tells us the military is after a formal and direct and explicit voice in policy-making—not just a major say in implementation. And that could mean, if it happens, a new centralization and consolidation of power far more portentous than are represented in the military-industrial complex.

It is possible, as Just allows, that such a change would prevent another Vietnam. There are a good many officers who want out of Vietnam at least as badly as the New Left. But it might also create four or five Vietnams. Even if the balance proved favorable, it would be the worst possible way to achieve such results. For it would erase forever the constitutional principle and the traditional practice of civilian control of the military. (And, as Gray observes, even one more Vietnam would finish us as a society capable of restoring its health.)

We are at the same point in dealing with the military, that is to say, as we are in confronting poverty, racial

[5] Just, *Military Men*, p. 206.

antagonisms, urban decay, educational malaise, and environmental pollution. There is a great temptation to resort to a gimmick for a quick and painless solution: to resolve an excruciating dilemma the way Oppenheimer did when confronted with the question of the H-bomb—by surrendering to the seduction of the "technically sweet" answer. But the truth is this: while the military has many weaknesses and numerous faults, and has made countless mistakes and has often pocketed any authority lying around unattended, the civilians have so far had the final responsibility. Hence dealing with the military begins and ends in dealing with civilians. Meaning dealing with ourselves and our spokesmen.

It *can* be done, though it clearly is becoming ever more difficult because we have lost so much of our willingness to confront the irrelevance of old ideas and to acknowledge our mistakes. Our vaunted pragmatism has almost withered in the heat of our passion for dogma. But we can gain some insight (and perhaps encouragement) by reviewing the careers of Generals MacArthur and Eisenhower. They offer a preview of the two courses we have before us: the politicizing of the military or the recommitment of the military to the primacy of the civilians (through a renewed engagement of the civilians in governing themselves).

The vital point about MacArthur is that he wanted to be Emperor rather than General. His dream was an extreme and intensely personalized version of the approach advanced more cautiously to Ward Just: the President would consult himself as Chief of Staff on the military aspects of his foreign policy. (In the third person, of course.) Let Eisenhower tell it: MacArthur disconcerted everyone because "he talked of himself in the third person," and if he "ever recognized the existence of that line [between the military and politics], he usually chose to ignore it."[6]

MacArthur is a classic example of the danger inherent in giving middle-class sons the idea that they can and should become gentlemen aristocrats or patricians or lords of the manor by way of military service. One is tempted to conclude that the deadly fault of laissez-faire capitalism was its inherent propensity to distort honest ambition into a commitment to known delusion. All that said, MacArthur played it straight and came as close to truth as his particular delusion would permit: he preferred to fade away rather than to fail in an attempt to become President. No pretender worth his ego will ever allow himself to be voted down by the friends of a haberdasher. Particularly after he has sacked a real and reactionary Emperor and then made himself into an icon of reform.

No doubt of it, MacArthur had an instinct for the viscera. Dominate The Corps at West Point, polish your already intense personal style, push your way into action assignments, make connections with politically influential senior officers, get into combat and lead your men in firefights, be sure you never receive the orders you know will stop you from routing the Bonus Army, do not stick your career into the cockpit of a tank or an airplane when all your superiors honor the infantry and the artillery, resign just before you know you will be needed in a major war, destroy the motor centers of the Japanese Empire and ignore the secondary twitching, revitalize the ene-

---

[6] Eisenhower, *At Ease*, pp. 213-214.

my you have defeated, and if you go for broke (the Presidency) always have a pocketful of poise (a corporation).

An awesome and commanding figure—yet flawed. Everyone, I suppose, has the urge to explain it all as the effect of mother. She surely was there. Everywhere. Always. Even after she died. But I think not. She was just the symbol of the real force at work: the desperate effort of the class conscious American middle class to put it all together. To get into the upper class as a wielder of power. Not prestige. Not money. Power: to act upon instead of being acted on. And values: to use the power for *The Good*. James presents much of this in a low key, but you feel it the way your lungs tell you—even before the barometer—about the coming of a storm at sea or on the prairie. Lovely work.

MacArthur's grandfather made it to the fringes of power through politics; he had a bit of early luck, a good mind, and great energy. But, as usual, there was no way to hand on what substance had been gained. The first son (MacArthur's father) had to earn it all over again, driven forward by the family heritage—that burr under the psyche—created by the grandfather. It was "one of nobility: A MacArthur is a man of superior mind and talents, a potential master of sundry fields; a MacArthur commands the respect of important personages at the highest levels of government and society; a MacArthur, by virtue of his family's high rank in the Scottish aristocracy of blood and the American aristocracy of success and wealth, is obligated to conduct himself with honor, gallantry, and magnanimity."[7]

---

[7]James, *The Years of MacArthur*, p. 11.

No way for MacArthur's father to honor *all that* in 1861 except by going to war. He could not even wait for an appointment to The Point or Annapolis. A brave and able soldier, and a leader, he chose the regular army instead of the law. His ambition, patience, ability, and performance carried him onto that marshy land of imperial administration in the Philippines after the Spanish-American War and the suppression of the rebellion. But William Howard Taft found him "politely lacking in any great consideration for the view of anyone, as to the real situation, who is a civilian." Elihu Root had to beat back his opposition to reform programs; and Theodore Roosevelt slapped him down for intruding into foreign policy matters.[8] Finally, Taft called his bluff to retire and sent him home to Milwaukee without any duties.

Once again there was nothing to sustain and develop—or to hand on. It had to be done again.

And so the next son, Douglas, started down the same road with even heavier freight: in addition to the heritage and the necessity, he carried, as James nicely puts it, his father's "disdain and contempt for civilian officials who interfered in what he considered to be his domain, and, a corollary, his own outspokenness on matters beyond his jurisdiction."[9] When one thinks soberly about a man sitting on that combination of personal and social dynamite, and somehow keeping it under control for more than fifty years, one has to touch one's cap.

But one also has to watch such a man. Certainly West Point did not tame that intense and pyramided ambition

---

[8] Ibid., pp. 39-41.

[9] Ibid., p. 44.

or socialize that sense of mission. The nation (let alone the Army) becomes a stage, and he who wants the lead is constantly trying to get his pencil into the script. Mac-Arthur managed a good bit of that, moreover, but not when he encountered men who understood and honored the traditions and practices of the Army and the country. When limits were set and enforced, and when he was given specific assignments, he could be exceptional. But he was always on the prowl for more influence, and always pushing to widen the theater of action.

Some of his constant and almost frenetic reconnaissance can be understood as part of a dedication to pulling the Army out of its long night as the second service. Even its gains during World War I were quickly lost, and it staggered through the 1920s and most of the 1930s as an organization that spent most of its money on nonmilitary programs. Men far less imperial than MacArthur became lonely, weary, discouraged, and frustrated.[10] But the best of them did what they could to prepare the way for the new weaponry, and they did not wander the border between soldiering and politics.

---

[10]The evidence on this part of the experience of the regular officer is overwhelming, even wrenching. The hazing at the academy must have seemed in retrospect like a harmless romp; and the women would have wept in laughter—or gone into hysterics—at the complaints of the modern housewife. Jack D. Foner (*The United States Soldier Between Two Wars: Army Life and Reforms, 1865-1898*, Humanities Press, 1970) deals with it during the earlier period (and its relationship to overbearing behavior by officers and to desertion), and there are moving accounts in James, in Ike's volume of reminiscences, and in Just's interviews with men returned from Vietnam.

Yet the striking thing is that MacArthur was never able to break free *except as civilians defined the situation in a way that opened the door to unlimited military action.* Even Philippine President Manuel L. Quezon, who granted his request for the title of Field Marshal, generally controlled his routine maneuverings and quietly set aside his grandiose plans. MacArthur's three key opportunities emerged out of a conception of the world which viewed America as threatened by an implacable and total challenge.

The first was the misreading of the Bonus March by President Herbert Hoover and others in the government. Those men came to see it as the potential or actual cutting edge of a revolutionary uprising. MacArthur was sure of that analysis and seized the opportunity to make policy as Chief of Staff. But he went too far and lost whatever chance he had to win popular acclaim; and his overbold action may well have cost him any chance to realize his dream, for it alerted Franklin Delano Roosevelt and other civilians to his overt ambition and his latent ruthlessness. Roosevelt played him as carefully as a trophy swordfish: absorbing his skill and energy in the CCC and in staff planning, and then landing him high and dry in the Philippines.

But then came the war against Facism and Imperial Japan, and Roosevelt's doctrine of unconditional surrender opened an even greater vista on political leadership. MacArthur leap-frogged along in the Pacific islands, gathering all the considerable power and prestige he could find, and served an amazing apprenticeship for the Presidency as *de facto* ruler of postwar Japan. Perhaps by then it was simply too late to move on to the White House.

More likely, the Korean War trapped him in the dilemma posed by the civilian demand, on the one hand, for implacable prosecution of the Holy Cold War against the infidels without, on the other hand, using all the power available.

President Truman and his hardline advisers like Dean Acheson, Clark Clifford, and John Foster Dulles not only defined foreign affairs in terms of a global crusade, but clearly attempted in Korea to act on the roll-back (or liberationist) principle that was implicit in the policy of containment. They planned to destroy the North Korean regime and unify the country under American hegemony. MacArthur would have accomplished that mission if the Chinese had not intervened, and he was understandably angry when his civilian superiors, who had given him the orders, refused to face the contradiction in their policy.

He dramatized the situation in his inimitable way: let me do what is necessary to accomplish what you say you want, or remove me from command. His failure, of course, was to omit the third option: re-evaluate what you want. If he had offered that, and tied it to his occasional rhetoric about the need to take a great risk for peace, he might very well have gone to the White House instead of Eisenhower. But MacArthur was as blind to that choice as the civilian superiors he challenged. That enabled them to fire him and struggle on with their crusade. Which is what they did. Which is why we are in Vietnam. And now the contradiction has come unraveled for all to see. Which is why the military is moving in on the decisions about what we want. One of the specters haunting us today is the ghost of MacArthur claiming his most important victory.

Perhaps Eisenhower can help us avoid that fate. He, too, had an instinct for the viscera: understand who you are and be true to that knowledge. Play no games. Do not scramble around on a bean stalk reputed to top out among the upper class. Honor the soldier's code to do the best you can with what the civilians hand you, and recognize and accept the limits of power (including your own). Even more than MacArthur, Eisenhower makes you wonder about West Point. It failed to make MacArthur responsible and it failed to overawe Eisenhower. What you go in with appears to be more important that what happens to you while you are there. Perhaps the only "West Point officers" are the young men who enter with no idea of who they are, and hence emerge as workaday careerists.

Reading Eisenhower's papers, including the book of correspondence with Chief of Staff George C. Marshall that Johns Hopkins Press has extracted from them, left me with a strange montage of images in my mind. There was Ike, calmly saying no to Winston Churchill's demand to end World War II by forming a skirmish line for World War III in Berlin (by-the-by explaining to the prime minister that it would be more helpful, if you could, Sir, to prod Field Marshal Montgomery north to Denmark before the Red Army got there moving west). I thought of John Quincy Adams saying no to Texas and advising his countrymen not to lose their souls on a trip abroad in search of monsters to destroy. There was Ike struggling to keep Georgie Patton on a working leash because he felt he had to have him if he could control him—and I thought, well, maybe that is the key to his later relationship with John Foster Dulles. Perhaps it was Ike, rather than the cancer, that mellowed the Bishop of Roll Back.

But mostly I thought of those exquisite essays that William Carlos Williams wrote about George Washington and Aaron Burr.[11] An eerie hour. For there is Eisenhower as twin brother to Washington—perhaps not a great soldier, but nevertheless an effective one; the language of the barracks and the natural modesty, reserve, and dignity; farmer shrewd and yet too trusting; not understanding the needs or the dynamic of civilian government, yet knowing the great truth that it was time to climb down off the White Charger; and sometimes exasperating in his patience and prudence. But then there is Ike as Aaron—writing his son that he loves him, saying honestly, "Do as you will," and advising him to ignore what "They say"; striking hard at special privileges for officers; taking risks beyond most of us; full of life to dance a pretty woman dizzy and to thumb his nose at protocol and authority; and in the end insisting that only the people can create a society fit for themselves and their children.

Altogether a more engaging and more creative and more human—and, yes, more challenging—man than MacArthur. And perhaps even a great soldier in the narrow professional sense. Certainly he saw and acted on the importance of tanks and planes before MacArthur. And he neither flinched nor floundered during the Battle of the Bulge, immediately taking charge and directing the counterattack. One of the things that Stephen Ambrose does very well in his study of Eisenhower as *Supreme Commander* (and he does a good many) is to clarify the

---

[11]Williams, *In The American Grain* (New Directions, 1956), pp. 140-143, 188-207.

nature of the European war. Whereas MacArthur was grossly overconfident in May, 1941, Eisenhower understood that it would be an extremely bitter struggle and from the outset recognized that Russia held the key to victory.

For that reason, Eisenhower (and Marshall) militantly opposed all peripheral campaigns. They fought long and hard for a commitment to go ashore in Europe in 1942, arguing that that was the only way to help Russia and weaken Germany. Roosevelt and Churchill overruled them, and the African campaign (Ike called it "a sideshow") led willy-nilly into the Italian morass. As a result, the decisive assault was delayed for two years. Even so, it was by no means a sure thing.

Ambrose faults Eisenhower for lacking a "ruthless, driving force"; but I think that judgment may be wide of the mark.[12] First of all, he could be—and was—implacable when he deemed it necessary. Secondly, he could not direct tactical combat in the field and also honor his strategic responsibilities as supreme commander. Nevertheless, he used his Pattons (*nobody* has many of them!) with an instinct for the jugular. Finally, he simply did not have the overwhelming force that is required to be ruthless in the sense that Ambrose invokes that criterion. Patton did run out of gas; and, in any event (as everyone knew), his tanks were no match in a one-to-one shoot-out with the Panthers or Tigers.[13]

---

[12] Ambrose, *Supreme Commander*, p. 137.

[13] Eisenhower, *Dear General*, p. 218. Eisenhower tried, whenever he could, to obtain such firsthand reports on combat. All these authors talk a good deal about the intense comradeship of com-

The hard truth of it, moreover, is that Eisenhower had a gut battle with the strategic air command, which was trying to do in World War II what it has done in Vietnam. The crucial difference was that Eisenhower's "ruthless, driving force" beat them down. The lightning-bolt boys did not want to mount a major campaign to bomb the French transportation system before D-Day, and displayed their usual mastery of the arrogantly false syllogism by arguing that such raids would kill too many civilians. They preferred their grotesque assault on industrial centers. Had they had their way then, as they have had in Vietnam, the 1,000 Year Reich might still be in business.

And if Ward Just is correct, then the moral of the story is the same for the military as it is for the civilian critics of the military. He reports that Vietnam is to be understood as a story of men who, having faced the *very delicate and scary balance in Normandy*, drew the conclusion that "World War Two . . . was one big engineering project. . . . Nothing is impossible for the United States if the country has the will and is prepared to pay the price

---

bat, but it is clear that the tensions and responsibilities of high command generate a similar involvement. James tries hard to communicate this feeling in his chapters on MacArthur's frontline experience in World War I, and Ambrose has some fine accounts of the love-anger outbursts between Eisenhower and various associates. But in truth, the novelist is the only one who has any real chance to give us either the essence or the substance of that experience. Two neglected gems are Glen Sire, *The Deathmakers* (Simon & Schuster, 1960), about a Pattonesque tank column in Europe, and Peter Bowman, *Beach Red* (Random House, 1945), about friendship and death during the first hour of an island operation in the Pacific. On war itself, Sire is better than Mailer.

in money and men."[14] Meaning that the contemporary military thinks that technology and the assembly line won World War II. But that seems almost certainly not the case in the sense that they mean it.

After the Russians, that is to say, the war was far more likely won by Eisenhower's determined application of *the force he had available* in a steady pressure that seemed cautious or hesitant only because it proceeded with the quiet of the tide. He maneuvered the Germans into defeat and surrender without a mass army—the Russians had twice as many men available for the assault on Berlin, for example, and their tanks could come down the middle of the street looking for Panthers and Tigers.

Eisenhower understood all that, and the awareness informed his later effort as Chief of Staff to extend and improve the coordination between civilian and military efforts for preparedness. Seymour Melman interprets that action (specifically Ike's directive of April 27, 1946) as founding the military-industrial complex that Eisenhower later warned about in his Farewell Address of January 17, 1961.[15] That makes for a nice bit of irony, but it will hardly do as history. The military-industrial complex, as Sidney Lens understands, goes back to Franklin Delano Roosevelt's close and continuing reliance on big business leaders throughout the Depression, and specifically to his use of Dollar-A-Year men to organize the economy for World War II.[16] The military-industrial complex is but

---

[14] Just, *Military Men*, p. 12.

[15] Melman, *Pentagon Capitalism*, vii, Appendix A.

[16] Lens, *Military-Industrial Complex*, pp. 12, 17-18. And on back,

one facet of the industrial-political conglomerate that has dominated the political economy throughout the twentieth century.

Melman is correct in arguing that the Pentagon Division of the Leviathan finally acquired a degree of autonomy, and his description of how it operates is a significant contribution to our understanding of the late twentieth-century political economy. But his analysis of how that degree of independence was gained is not particularly helpful because he dismisses the role of imperialism and overweights the importance of an "institutionalized power-lust."[17] Along with most observers who discount the importance of imperialism as a dynamic, causal element in modern American policy, Melman first stacks his argument by artifically defining imperialism as a matter of simplistic and wholly rational economic motives. Thus imperialism cannot explain Vietnam because "no one has demonstrated any past, present, or foreseeable volume of trade or investment in Vietnam and/or adjacent areas that would justify an outlay of $100 billion."[18]

Even with his own assumptions, however, Melman gives away too much in that sentence. There is abundant evidence that many leaders (and advisers) saw Vietnam as the key to Southeast Asia and viewed the resources of that region as crucial for the long-term functioning of the American political economy. They were no doubt mistaken, and many of them have changed their minds. But

I would add, to President Woodrow Wilson's similar approach during World War I.

[17] Melman, *Pentagon Capitalism*, p. 4.

[18] Ibid., pp. 7-8, 155-156.

neither consideration alters the fact that imperial calcula-tions have a role in the making of policy. Melman sees how important national economic considerations are for understanding the rise of state-management in the Penta-gon. What is surprising is that he fails to recognize that the same kind of considerations came to supplement (though not wholly replace) the individualized economic motive that was significant in building the empire. Main-taining an empire is a different kind of operation from building one, but that does not mean that it ceases to be imperialism—or that economic concerns lose their influ-ence.

Lens makes this point very nicely in reviewing how President Harry S Truman, Dean Acheson, and countless others defined the Holy Cold War in terms of "free enter-prise," the "problem of markets," and the apocalyptic certainty that the American system "could survive in America only if it became a world system."[19] Such men insisted that freedom and prosperity at home were de-pendent upon establishing, preserving, and extending them abroad—in American terms. There is no way—repeat, no way—to saddle the military with the responsibility for that conception of reality. True enough, the military was ready to serve as a true believer, but it did not define the world in such ways and it did not then cast policy in military terms. One need not (indeed, should not) accept at face value George Frost Kennan's effort to extricate himself from a significant share of the responsibility for that culminating debacle. But his account in his memoirs of the rapid and thorough way in which civilians en-

---

[19]Lens, *Military-Industrial Complex*, pp. 22-23.

couraged militarization of foreign policy is convincing beyond a doubt. As are countless other documents.

In that important sense, the officers interviewed by Ward Just make a central point. "The thing goes back to the President, who is the commander in chief, and the population that elected him. . . . If you get into the wrong war that's not the fault of the Army."[20] "It is the civilians who should be called into account, because it is the civilians who permitted the process to spin out of control. . . . The military man still believes what he hears from the White House and from the Vice President: to wit, Communism is a menace and the United States has the right and duty to oppose it."[21] You know. Like John Fitzgerald Kennedy said: The United States is prepared to "pay any price, bear any burden" in defense of "the free world," so "ask not what your country can do for you, but . . ." etc.

That brings us full circle, back to Gray and the questions of war and guilt. But first a final note about Eisenhower. *He alone cooled it down*. The boy from Kansas may not have been properly ruthless, and no doubt failed to force through all the reforms that were desirable, but at crucial moments he could and did speak two very important words: "Enough" and "No." No doubt he should have said them more often; and then gone on in other matters to cry "Yes" and "More." But he turns out to have been saner than either his immediate predecessors or successors in the White House.

So there we are: there simply is no easy answer to the

---

[20] Just, *Military Men*, pp. 13-14.

[21] Ibid., pp. 182-183.

problem of the military in a society struggling to govern itself. Cutting the military in on policy-making is like inviting the cat to give the canary a bath. You might find a few that would stand guard against the bird dogs, but in between you would lose control of the house. It would be more realistic to insist that the concept of Duty involve the practice of public resignation by military officers (and civilians) who conclude that their orders involve a contradiction in terms or a violation of their constitutional responsibilities. A good many young academy officers—and draftees—have had the courage to take that course, and it would help mightily if we honored them as grandly as we award those who have endured the horrors of combat. The mines laid by the forces of conformity split one just as terribly as those buried by any other enemy.

But for now that is a dream. A tradition of resignation from office that has real consequences is—or ought to be—one of the goals of the revolution. The important things for now are to distinguish between guilt and war crimes, to avoid scapegoating, and to get closer to the attitude that will enable us to make that "daring, voluntary, and decisive act of breaking the sword." As Gray understands, the sense of guilt that can truly make a difference is the one that can move each of us to acknowledge our own share in the disaster and then to join our neighbors in reasserting our power as citizens to change the outlook that has carried us to the very edge of catastrophe. Out of that can come an affirmation and a confidence that can build an American community.

It would be tragic to externalize all moral energy in a righteous trial of what we all now know is wrong. It is not really to the point to say simply that if all of us are guilty, then no one is guilty. The trouble is that when all of us are guilty we much prefer to shovel it all off on a few so we can go on with business as usual. It is time we recognized the potential health in honest guilt, acknowledged our mistakes, and healed ourselves through political action to create an America that will no longer be hated and feared. That is, incidentally, the only sure way to solve the problem of the military. And, also, the problem of law and order.

V

Ol' Lyndon—and JFK

The issue here is how we read a document. For how we read determines what we learn.

So far, at any rate, we have not been learning much from this slyly honest witness. Mostly we have heard a frustrated (and therefore angry) complaint that Ol' Lyndon did not go naked down to the river and confess his sins in chants of unconditional surrender. But then I remembered Abbie Hoffman's belated admission that Revolution for the Hell of It is a contradiction in terms, and it struck me that Lyndon went to the river before Abbie. I have a feeling that the comparison may tell us as much about the weakness of the left during its most striking opportunity since it blew the Great Depression as all the books that will ever be written on the subject.

We face, on another front, the precious vanguard of sophisticated nags who fill the page with put-downs of the man. They scan the document to cull footnotes for a priori conclusions of such profundity as that LBJ was not JFK. My, how the computers must be overheating under the load of all those Brownie Points coming in from the Ivy League. The one relevant aspect of John Kenneth Galbraith's egoistic digression is his honesty about the

---

The Vantage Point: Perspectives of the Presidency, 1963-1969 by Lyndon Baines Johnson (Holt, Rinehart & Winston).

supercilious arrogance of such elitist evasions.[1] If the Liberal Establishment were prepared to lead us plebs into the Golden Age, it would have neither the time nor the need to belabor Lyndon and his merely human torments. Having won the battle at the crossroads with their shiny new crossbows, the prodigies would be fingering the Grail.

Alas.

Rather, thank God. (Remember the Bay of Pigs, the Green Berets, the Missile Madness, and the noble call to Define Ourselves in Terms of the State?)

Next there will be many readers of the witness who will try to use it as the cornerstone for their own ambitious architecture. You know: the dreary academic-bureaucratic strategy of constructing one's own career upon a critique of another's labor. If you have that much leisure, and are hung up on reading, you can relax about what to do for the next decade.

So we are left with the most difficult alternative (there *is* a double meaning there, but it will have to wait for another essay). The only way forward is to make the effort to read with skepticism, compassion, and a readiness to recognize a truth we did not expect to find. That is, try to be a historian. Or, if you (like me) prefer the idiom of Thucydides, try to be a citizen. Meaning read Lyndon to understand better what we have wrought, and how we misbent the iron, in order to undo what we came to feel (when manipulated through appeals to our good intentions and our egos) was our finest hour.

Extremely difficult and terribly painful.

---

[1] J. K. Galbraith, "Seeing Things Through for JFK," *Saturday Review* (November 6, 1971).

But Lyndon has given us some leverage, and it is crucial to use it carefully: "I make no pretense of having written a complete and definitive history of my Presidency. I have tried, rather, to review that period from a President's point of view—reflecting a President's personal and political philosophy. . . . I have not written these chapters to say, 'This is how it was,' but to say, 'This is how I saw it from my vantage point.' "[2]

That is an honest and basically accurate description of his book *The Vantage Point*. It is not in any sense a complete account of his Presidency, even from his point of view, and some of the gaps (as in the treatment of civil rights, black-white relations, and crime) are so panoramic as to remind one of Johnson's own ranch. But therein lies the essential usefulness of the volume: it is conclusive evidence of how the Vietnam War had fuzzed his mind. At the end of his tenure he saw everything as skewed by the pain of that traumatic wound to his conception of America. Just so: his distorted vision should help us see clearly how our imperial foreign policy has twisted our best perceptions and subverted our good intentions, and thereby carried us to the edge of disaster.

In a very real sense, that is, Johnson is telling us, however unconsciously or indirectly, about how our failure to sustain and extend the social movement created by Eugene Debs left us with nothing but the traditional solution to our problems: open the door to another frontier while defending those already settled. For that is the only possible way to sustain market place liberalism. Johnson happened to be the man who was President when that

---

[2] Johnson, *The Vantage Point*, p. ix.

truth worked itself out in front of our eyes—and with our lives.[3]

But Johnson tells us even more. He gives us a crucial insight into what it means to be a white Southerner who accepts and tries to adapt to the victory of the North. For he saw first and always as a *Southern* white who grew up wandering hither and yon across that no-man's land that divides the lowers from the maybe middles. He knew want and work, and learned what the constancy of both did to his parents and his neighbors. That prism-prison distorts some truths, but it clarifies others that the rest of us seldom glimpse—let alone see and feel and therefore know.

One of those is an excruciating awareness of the rest of the country's pervasive anger and contempt toward the South (that backward slough). Acknowledge and live with that truth as a Northern white and you begin to understand Johnson.[4] The visceral essay on the white Southerner as a second-class citizen has yet to be written. C. Vann Woodward is just too damn polite. And Norman Mailer has not considered it important enough. But if you wonder about their hawkish bellicosity, for example, remember that they alone among us have been defeated and occupied, and then kept down economically, politically, and emotionally for yet another century.

---

[3] I considered these points to be obvious, or at any rate clearly implied by the rest of my remarks, when I first wrote this essay. I have made them explicit because some readers seemed to think I was apologizing for Johnson when instead I was—and am—trying to indicate in a humane way how we can all learn from his terror and failure.

[4] Johnson, *The Vantage Point*, pp. 18, 89, 95, 155.

Then put that Southern consciousness of being first among the damned into a male with a great and earthy zest for life who has suffered a heart attack; and then make that man President because the young and handsome symbol of Northern power and smug self-satisfaction has been murdered while visiting a backward and unruly Southern fief. I think you have to take that man seriously when he says he was of a mind not to tempt the gods in 1964. Of course he was torn. Hell, yes, he wanted victory in his—and his beloved South's—own right, but I have a strong sense that he would have gone home if Lady Bird had said the bags were packed. Her lines about becoming the handy dart board for all the tension and anger, and about the drinking, are masterpieces: the South is *finally here* and the sex is going, Love; so if you do not challenge Fate, the booze will get you. In that league, Ms. Camelot is a spectator who does not even know the name of the game. It sure as hell is not touch football.

I am glad he stayed. That does not mean I like what happened. I am glad he stayed because what he did at home (especially in trying openly to help the blacks and the poor), and what he did in Vietnam after the attack on the Marines at Danang, finally brought us to the visceral confrontation with ourselves that offers us a chance to break out of our traditional outlook. Given all that has gone before, I do not think that option could open up in any other way. And the Kennedys (and maybe even another white Northern Establishment man) might well have finessed the mess into another classic American victory.

Dear God.

It is easy to discount Johnson's concern and determination to help the poor and the old and the other put-downs. You have heard it many times: "Oh, that just comes naturally to a populist." But many poor boys— probably most—forget those other people once they scratch and claw their way into the front row at the feed trough. The primary issue here, though it takes a bit of care to confront it directly, is how the programs reveal the limits of white Northern liberalism. We must begin, though, with Johnson's knowledge of how to move the system. That was the product of his white Southern experience: if they will not let you run it from the top, then learn how to control it from the side. Others from the South could have maneuvered the legislative victories just about as effectively if they had cared. And, so far as *whites* are concerned, some of them do care.

So the populist answer is not enough. For Johnson included the blacks and other nobodies. Not just up *to* the crunch, but *through* the crunch. The way he tells us how he began to transcend the color line is beautiful. His black driver asked him (after he had become a member of the Congress) to stop taking the dog along on the numerous trips back and forth to Texas. It was hard enough, he explained, just barrelin' through in three days. But a black man was utterly beaten down because of all those extra hours spent looking for a place to piss—let alone to eat and sleep—and it was just too damn much, even if you are a good man, Mr. Lyndon, for a black man with a dog. And his soul confrontation with his fellow white Southerners during an address to the Congress remains a great moment.[5]

---

[5]Ibid., pp. 154-155; then see pp. 29, 39, 73, 157.

"What happened in Selma is part of a far greater movement which reaches into every section and state of America. It is the effort of American Negroes to secure for themselves the full blessings of American life."

I paused for breath. In that fleeting moment my thoughts turned to the picket line in Birmingham, the sit-ins in North Carolina, the marches in Selma. . . .

I raised my arms.

"Their cause must be our cause too. Because it is not just Negroes, but really it is all of us who must overcome the crippling legacy of bigotry and injustice. And . . . we . . . shall . . . overcome."

And here, in this memoir, he does what few other whites of any section have done. He admits publicly that he was wrong about black power. No radical chic here: just poor white Southerner gittin' on down the line.[6]

When asked about black power in 1966, I responded: "I am not interested in black power or white power. What I am concerned with is democratic power, with a small *d*." As I look back now, that answer seems totally insufficient. It is easy for a white man to say he is "not interested in black power or white power." Black power had a different meaning to the black man, who recently had had to seek the white world's approval and for whom success had come largely on white people's terms. To such a man, black power meant a great deal—in areas that mattered the most—dignity, pride, and self-awareness.

---

[6]Ibid., first see pp. 155-162 and 164-165; then p. 167.

What we come down to, then, are the concepts that guided Ol' Lyndon. And those were the product of orthodox Northern white liberalism. The program was simply the ideas of the New and Fair Deals pushed to their limits. And, underlying all, the American Zen Buddhism of *growth*. The nonviolent, nondisruptive way to solve all problems. "The economic pie was big enough for everyone—and growing much faster than our population."[7] But it did not work for Franklin Delano Roosevelt or Harry S Truman, and it did not work for Lyndon Baines Johnson.

This fallacy is tucked away in the classical capitalist assumption (and prayer) that growth will mask the inequitable and irrational use and distribution of resources, as well as meet the demands of increasing population and the cry from everyone for more goodies. Another difficulty was that not even Ol' Lyndon could forever override the Southerners and Northerners who demanded duly sanitized and processed representatives when the past seemed about to push us into the present in such matters as community initiative and control of community affairs.[8] But the gut truth of it is that the Great Society was what Franklin Roosevelt should have proposed in 1936. It was too little and too late in 1963.

None of that can be dumped on Lyndon. Unless, of course, you simply prefer your rulers to spend their childhood in upstate New York or Cape Cod rather than in Texas. Only a thimbleful of radicals and utopians were offering anything significantly more imaginative and fundamental. If the Great Society was Camelot's program,

[7]Ibid., p. 30.
[8]Ibid., p. 83.

then the New Frontier was nothing more than the liberal intellectuals whoopin' it up back at The Old Stamping Ground.[9] If it was mostly Johnson, as I think it was, then he deserves credit for striving to do all that was possible within the orthodoxy he had been taught.

In any event, it was Johnson rather than Kennedy who moved the system. The Kennedy machine was like a freeway cruiser: beautiful on the way to the White House or the moon, but of little help in getting coal to Grandma in the snow. A full appreciation of Lyndon's contraption, which would make either kind of trip, depends upon an understanding of two of the assumptions behind the Constitution.

One holds that the Constitution enables a majority (even a strong plurality) of the people to do almost anything they want to do if and when they function as citizens. The other promises that when the people do not act as citizens nothing terribly bad can happen because of the carefully designed structural baffles (and the size of the empire) that prevent any man or group from appropriating total power, and because the government will in any event be managed in trust by the best available men who sit in the Senate and the White House. The first proposition is largely true. The second is demonstrably false. And therein lies the trouble.

Johnson does not discuss the problem in those formal terms in *The Vantage Point* (though I have little doubt

---

[9]Here the mind-bending essay is W. I. Susman, "The Persistence of American Reform," in *American Reform: The Ambiguous Legacy*, edited by D. Walden (Yellow Springs, Ohio: The Ampersand Press, 1967), pp. 94-108.

that he could). But he does let us see what happens when the people stay home glued to the tube. It is very simple. The men charged with the responsibilities in the Senate and the White House have to distort and manipulate (and thereby weaken) the basically representative system to cope with immediate needs and to try to fulfill the public's expression of its wishes when it last performed as an assembly of citizens.

All very understandable. And all very dangerous. First, it means that the honest custodians have to bargain in a closed environment (the Congress) with other minds closed to almost everything except the bullheaded self-interest of those who define citizenship as die-hard protection of their self-defined welfare. Second, the powers of the Presidency are fudged and fudged again in order to do what the sometime citizenry said it wanted during its last venture into self-government. It all comes down to creeping benevolent despotism—with serious limits on the opportunity to be benevolent.

Very bad news. Even if (as with Johnson) your hero is Franklin Roosevelt.[10] Perhaps particularly if Roosevelt is your patron saint. For that means *you* as acolyte have to develop on your own the inner strength to engage the people in serious dialogue when they finally arouse themselves as citizens. Franklin is a poor guide for that trip. A dialogue is not a Fireside Chat. He never said anything as gutsy about the blacks as Lyndon did—or did anything as meaningful to help them. And Roosevelt set the pattern for easing the nation into war through disingenuous maneuvers.[11]

---

[10] Johnson, *The Vantage Point*, pp. 70, 81, 104, 324, 327, 345.

[11] Or was it Wilson?

So we come to Vietnam (and the Dominican Republic).

Remember whom we have at the bar. A Southern poor white who molded himself in the image of an upstate New York aristocrat and *that* kind of *noblesse oblige*, and then came to power because a Massachusetts *nouveau riche* (and *that* kind of pseudo *noblesse oblige*) had been killed in the heart of his own Texas. Foreign policy offers such a man the *one and only* basis for taking the oath with any confidence that he is truly an American in his own right. Foreign policy is the magic key. For there he *is* in tune. He is a child of his age.

Lyndon's critics are wrong. He was not unprepared for foreign policy, he was instead miseducated with masterful efficiency by the white Northern elite that had dominated the conduct of foreign affairs since 1865.

> Like most men and women of my generation, I felt strongly that World War II might have been avoided if the United States in the 1930s had not given such an uncertain signal of its likely response to aggression in Europe and Asia.

Then consider the projection of that outlook in his May 23, 1961, report to Kennedy on his mission to Asia.

> 1. The battle against Communism must be joined in Southeast Asia with strength and determination to achieve success there—or the United States, inevitably, must surrender the Pacific and take up our defenses on our own shores.... 3. There is no alternative to United States leadership in Southeast Asia.... 8. ... The basic decision in Southeast Asia is here. We must decide whether to help these

countries to the best of our ability or throw in the towel in the area and pull back our defenses to San Francisco and a "Fortress America" concept.[12]

Along the way, the teaching continued. After Roosevelt, the instructor was Truman. The haberdasher as town tutor: bringing the insights of Wilson and the two Roosevelts to Main Street.

It must be the policy of the United States to support free peoples who are resisting attempted subjugation by armed minorities or by outside pressure. . . . We must assist free peoples to work out their own destinies in their own way. . . . Collapse of free institutions and loss of independence would be disastrous not only for them but for the world.[13]

Our foreign relations, political and economic, are indivisible. . . . We are the giant of the economic world. . . . The choice is ours. . . . So our devotion to freedom of enterprise, in the United States, has deeper roots than a desire to protect the profits of ownership. It is part and parcel of what we call American.[14]

The various elements in that outlook, first brought together by Wilson, were tightly integrated by the white Northern elite in National Security Council Document 68 (prepared during the winter of 1949-1950). The gospel as amended and interpreted by Dean G. Acheson, associated bishops, and consulting Protestant Jesuits. If the true

---

[12]Johnson, *The Vantage Point*, p. 46, 147-148; *The Pentagon Papers* (Bantam, 1971), pp. 128-129.

[13]Truman, March 12, 1947 (The Truman Doctrine).

[14]Truman, March 6, 1947 (address at Baylor University).

American faith is to be maintained and advanced, "the nation must be determined, at whatever cost or sacrifice, to preserve at home and abroad those conditions of life in which those objectives can survive and prosper." The United States will be the sun, "with other free nations in variable orbits around it." This "means the virtual abandonment by the United States of trying to distinguish between national and global security. . . . Security must henceforth become the dominant element in the national budget, and other elements must be accommodated to it."[15] Underlying it all, of course, were the assumptions that Washington was the Holy See of the new empire and that America possessed the necessary power.

Here again, as with the explanation of Johnson as populist, we need to move carefully to undo the facile, unfair, and misleading charges that Vietnam was Johnson's war. First, it is impossible to separate domestic from foreign affairs. Second, NSC-68 is the classic expression of the American projection of that truth into absurdity: for America to be well, the entire world must take the patented American remedy and then follow the American diet. Third, the absurdity cannot be laid in the lap of Lyndon Baines Johnson. Even Townsend Hoopes acknowledges that Johnson was educated in that idiom and that Kennedy bequeathed him advisers who thought "about the external world in the simplistic terms of appeasement versus military resolve."[16] Hoopes is so ex-

---

[15] C. Phillips, *The Truman Presidency: The History of a Triumphant Succession* (Macmillan, 1966), pp. 306-308.

[16] T. Hoopes, *The Limits of Intervention* (McKay, 1969), pp. 6-7, 15-16. But also see C. L. Cooper, *The Lost Crusade: America in Vietnam* (Dodd, Mead, 1970), p. 13.

cited, relieved, and impressed by his own awakening from the nightmare that he not only blames Johnson for the wrong things but totally ignores those brave souls who had been warning about the impending disaster through the long and lonely night. Finally, the major point is to learn from Johnson's sad experience in carrying the absurdity to its insane conclusion.

Truman took us a good way down that path by going to war in Korea without so much as a courtesy call on the Congress. The Congress seemed to have forgotten that he was supposed to come by, but that does not absolve HST. For a time, nothing happened. Then, slowly and cautiously, almost as though they were learning to walk after a year in traction, some Americans began to act as citizens. The ensuing protest against the Korean War was not dramatic, but it was significant and ultimately influential. The crucial weakness of that opposition was that it focused narrowly on the war rather than on the war as the expression of the underlying outlook of liberal capitalism.

Truman met no resistance as he simultaneously implemented the *Weltanschauung* in Indochina, even though the antiwar sentiment clearly affected the election of 1952.[17] Thus the possibility of a serious reconsideration of the traditional approach that would lead on to different action depended wholly upon the wild chance that the President, or a significant number of other established leaders, would be jarred enough by the war, or by the antiwar feeling, to question orthodox assumptions and policies.

---

[17]Cooper, *The Lost Crusade*, p. 63.

Wonder of wonders, a boy from Kansas who stayed human through West Point did gingerly approach that heresy. Dwight David Eisenhower occasionally talked bluntly in private about the possibility of direct intervention in Indochina (and allowed John Foster Dulles to preach about it far too much), but the key fact is that he acted very cautiously.[18] He made no irreversible commitment, and did not trap himself by exposing advisers to enemy fire. And there is something more: for, in spite of his failure to confront Joseph McCarthy quickly or decisively enough, he did not appease the wild man from Wisconsin by embarking on overseas adventures.

There was an important bit of Hoover in Eisenhower: the kind of perception, for example, that enabled Hoover to tell Truman in 1945 to relax and concentrate on improving life in the United States and the Western Hemisphere. And also the sense of proportion and confidence that allowed Ike to say simply that the United States should not overreact to criticism, or to annoying but secondary policy actions by other nations. For that matter, Hoover's strong attack of December 20, 1950, against the Truman approach was an important factor in opening the sometimes pointed discussion of global interventionism that set the background for the election of 1952; and once elected Eisenhower revealed himself in action to be far closer to Hoover than to Dulles.

John Fitzgerald Kennedy was of a different breed. He charged on to honor orthodoxy and to revive the activism of Truman. In foreign affairs, at any rate, he displayed little understanding of either the virtue or the sanity of

---

[18]Ibid., pp. 134-137.

going slow. Even of doing nothing. He agreed (in 1956) with Dulles that it would be wrong to hold elections throughout Vietnam. He described the make-believe government below the seventeenth parallel as the

> ... cornerstone of the Free World in Southeast Asia, the Keystone to the arch, the finger in the dike. ... Moreover, the independence of Free Vietnam is crucial to the free world in fields other than the military. Her economy is essential to the economy of all of Southeast Asia; and her political liberty is an inspiration to those seeking to obtain or maintain their liberty in all parts of Asia—and indeed the world. The fundamental tenets of this nation's foreign policy, in short, depend in considerable measure upon a strong and free Vietnamese nation.[19]

Four years later, campaigning against Richard Milhous Nixon, he attacked the Eisenhower failure to oust Fidel Castro as symptomatic of the Republican inability to deal toughly with Russia. Castro was "a source of maximum danger." "Those [like Nixon] who say they will stand up to Khrushchev have not demonstrated the ability to stand up to Mr. Castro." As for the main show, Kennedy argued that it was urgent to initiate a major increase in military spending because of the nature of the enemy and his great advantage in missiles: "There is very little time. The enemy is lean and hungry and the United States is the only strong sentinel at the gate."[20]

---

[19]Ibid., pp. 150, 168.

[20]Here I extend the original version of this essay to offer more information and to clarify rather cryptic discussions of several

Once elected, Kennedy quickly surrounded himself with zealous "watchmen on the walls of freedom" and launched a major effort to strengthen and refine the orthodox counterrevolutionary policy by applying the relevant manipulatory insights and techniques of the social sciences, and by adopting centralized and computerized management.[21] It may help in understanding Robert S. McNamara to approach him as the white Northern equivalent of Lyndon B. Johnson. That is, the white Northern middle-class boy who became corporation manager and then took on the challenge of controlling the military by asserting American control of the world without relying on the Joint Chiefs of Staff.

Jackie had hardly filled the second closet of her wardrobe before JFK was striding down the road that led to war in Vietnam. The first move involved Laos. Kennedy promptly defined that lovely lazy land as being essential to American security, and then began to act on that view with such a slow-witted analysis and heavy-handed interference that open military intervention was a real possibility for a period of months.

Next came the opening phase of the military build-up which, in spite of official admission that the missile gap

---

important points. The publishing schedule for this collection made it impossible to do that in an essay on R. J. Walton's *Cold War and Revolution: The Foreign Policy of John F. Kennedy* (Viking Press, 1972). Walton offers a coherent interpretation of Kennedy, though his major points have been presented by others in less integrated fashion. His sense of the meaning of Kennedy's famous speech at American University, however, is particularly keen.

[21] Cooper, *The Lost Crusade*, p. 207; A. Austin, *The President's War* (Lippincott, 1971), pp. 30-31.

did not exist, finally topped-out at about $6 billion. The first requests were made when Kennedy and his advisers interpreted Russia's exploratory bid to unfreeze the Berlin stalemate as posing a dire threat to the United States. More young men were requisitioned to serve the state in military tasks, more reserve units were activated, various regular units were placed on high alert, and a request for $207 million momentarily took the issue of civil defense out of mothballs. Happily, the Russians did not overreact in the same fashion.

Then came the Bay of Pigs. In view of all the debate about whether or not Kennedy would have walked on and on into the Vietnam quagmire (as Johnson did), it is fair to explore the question of Eisenhower and the exile force that he allowed Nixon and the Dulles Brothers to organize. My view is this: in the crunch Eisenhower would not have authorized an invasion. First, because of his aversion to armed intervention per se. Second, because his military expertise would have informed him that Castro did not pose a threat to the security of the United States. Third, because as an unusually sensitive and responsible commanding officer, he would not have sent 1,500 men on such an operation without American support. And fourth, the necessity of American involvement would have reinforced his deep reluctance to order more Americans to die.

Nixon is different. Scarily so. I am sure that in 1961 he would have gone in with everything required. Which would have been a hell-of-a-lot more than he would have assumed was necessary, and which might therefore have produced the first Vietnam. So give Kennedy his due: he did not do *that*.

But what Kennedy did do was considerably more than enough to warrant grave criticism; and his action surely trapped Johnson and the rest of us for what seems an eternity of shame and agony. The heart of the trouble was that Kennedy could not step back and put the relationship between Castro, the United States, and himself in perspective. There are several ways to explain it: if you are hooked on psycho-history, then it is the *machismo* rivalry (including Kennedy's uncertainty and insecurity about what to do inside the United States) that will strike you; if you stress ideology, then it is the faith in Christian corporate capitalism as the true and necessary way (Kennedy as Wilson); if you prefer class analysis it is the inability of any President, whatever his best intentions and hopes, to say no to the orthodoxies of corporate capitalism unless he has been elected by a social movement with strength and imagination; and if you emphasize politics, then it is a combination of knowing that Nixon probably *did* beat you in Illinois and Texas, and the necessity of honoring your rhetoric to establish your credibility in order to be re-elected.

Whichever of those options you choose, the central point here is that the Cuban Missile Crisis was a direct result of the Bay of Pigs. Kennedy did not learn from that error and failure. He did not let go. He lacked the imagination and courage to re-examine the white Northern liberal catechism and go to the people with a confession that would revive them as citizens. Instead, he took the by-pass. The cop-out in the guise of tough-mindedness: No More Cubas. As if a sane man would undertake always to win.

That made him a hostage of the right, and trapped him

[101]

into settling for less than his *own* aspirations. One undertakes to stay in power to do good for the people by drastically narrowing one's definition of the good. Thus Cuba remained under "our most careful surveillance." He gave serious consideration to any proposal that seemed likely to blot out the defeat. There was open talk of another invasion, and he persistently discussed the assassination of Castro.

Irony of ironies.

Terror of terrors.

Everyone who cared knew about those discussions. After all, you only had to read one of five: *The Nation*, *The New York Times*, *The Congressional Record*, *I. F. Stone's Weekly*, or the *Washington Post*. And if you had even the loosest kind of connection, you were privy to reputed (and undoubtedly distorted) quotations. Khrushchev and Castro had very good connections, and they were understandably and increasingly scared.

So they asked for assurances that there would be no reworked replay. Kennedy gave them nothing, not even the back of his mind. So then the missiles were moved in to italicize two points: revolutions in small countries are no longer the exclusive business of the United States, and we Russians think it is time you Americans also lived inside the parabola of nuclear missiles so that you will learn by doing (so to speak) that you are not unique.

The missiles, as Theodore C. Sorenson has so eloquently explained (McNamara and others were typically more prosaic in making the same point), "did not substantially alter the strategic balance *in fact*." At this point, given what we know, I think Khrushchev initially made one of two mistakes: either he overestimated Kennedy and assumed that the President would open private talks about Cuba and other matters; or he counted on the shock of the missiles to accomplish the same objective.

Either way, Khrushchev was wrong. But he adjusted quickly and effectively, realizing that Kennedy was not a man who was capable of making the first gesture. So he did. We are all indebted to Khrushchev for recognizing his man, and for being himself a human being able to accept what seemed to be a public defeat in order to attain important objectives.

The confrontation with Khrushchev may have been the most important, if limited, learning experience in the life of John Fitzgerald Kennedy. For he grasped the vital point that America was no longer a nation with the power to impose its will upon a small nation if another superpower takes the poor and the weak under its nuclear umbrella. Ike knew that, but he was not a teacher; and Kennedy's concept of courage was not sophisticated enough to include Hoover.

So it was Khrushchev who tutored Kennedy for the famous speech at American University. It was lovely. More beautiful than he realized, however, for while he publicly unzipped the Truman Doctrine as it affected direct confrontations between nuclear powers, he had not learned the other lesson from Cuba: a social movement can unzip a nuclear empire.

So on he went into Vietnam. "We are not going to withdraw" from Vietnam: "for us to withdraw . . . would mean a collapse not only of South Vietnam but Southeast Asia." Dominoes with a shot of Irish whisky. That crusading zeal manifested itself, sooner than later, in a steady expansion of American troops who were exposed to combat and who had been imbued with the true faith "to revolutionize the economy and political structure of the provinces . . . during their one-year tour of duty."[22] Read revolutionize to mean Americanize, and read advisers-in-the-field-exposed-to-enemy-fire to mean votes in the pocket of Barry M. Goldwater and Associates.[23] Kennedy had defined himself into the trap of having to win abroad to win at home.

That put Johnson in the position of a man wandering down an arroyo with a cloudburst moving in behind the hills. Given all the elements that had been unleashed, the wonder is that he went so slow.[24] It says a good bit about the man. True, I would not have gone at all, and of course neither would you, but that is not the issue. To stop at that point is to engage in the worst kind of self-indulgence.

So we are not yet done.

At a crucial juncture, Johnson did do less than was in him. I do not mean that I think he was capable of drawing on hidden and inner resources to transcend the outlook he had been taught and which he had internalized as his own. The point is that he did not honor, after the first direct attacks on American units, his own commitment to the existing system. That is the only solid ground for criticism. Meaning that it is so easy to fault a man for

---

[22]Cooper, *The Lost Crusade*, pp. 211, 207.

[23]Austin, *The President's War*, pp. 30, 43, 104. On the same trap in the Dominican Revolution, consult J. Slater, *Intervention and Negotiation* (Harper & Row, 1970), pp. 16-17, 32, 199. Then see *The Vantage Point*, pp. 19, 42, 197-198, 201-202, 280.

[24]Here *read The Lost Crusade*.

not breaking free of his own views that it is pointless. But it is something quite different when a man does not honor his own code.

There *were* excruciating circumstances. The assassination, and the coming to power as a proxy. And all those "advisers" in Vietnam, with ever more of them being killed. Johnson had not selected a single major adviser in America, and had not sent a single adviser to Vietnam. Even so, in spite of the liberal orthodoxy and the clamor from the right, those problems might have been fuzzed enough to fold the tent.

That became extremely difficult after the assassination and the nomination of Goldwater. Still, Johnson gave it a try. I do not think that the Tonkin Gulf Boo-Boo was the point of no return. Being an Academy man, I say simply that the Navy looks bad. We did fire first, and there is no such thing as a warning shot between two men of war.[25]

In the beginning, moreover, Johnson was not a Truman. Not even a Roosevelt. And certainly not a Kennedy saying yes to the Bay of Pigs in the secrecy of his clique. Johnson *did* go to the Congress. At that point, looking back, I think that all of us who defined the problem as centering on Johnson made the mistake of personalizing the political process. If we believe in self-government, that is to say, then we should insist upon the power of the representative bodies, and control them by our involvement as citizens, rather than lusting after a hero to whom we can hand over even more authority. And that means building a social movement to elect a man or woman of our persuasion instead of simply humiliating a man who is

---

[25] *The President's War*: it has to be read through.

the natural product of a system that we assume to be incapable of defining and dealing with the real problems.

If we are serious about radical reform (let alone revolution), then we need to become a bit more sophisticated about the North Vietnamese and the VC. They have every right to decide their own strategy and tactics. And we can wish them success within the framework of an honest (if disturbed) commitment to the principle of self-determination. But we also need to learn, for our own purposes, how the leaders of the Establishment respond to such a frontal challenge.

The February, 1965, decision by the North Vietnamese or the VC (or both) to mount persistent frontal attacks on American units is understandable. I might very well have supported the same policy if I had endured those previous twenty years as a Vietnamese. But there are many ways to win, and the key to choosing among them is a knowledge of one's opponent. And I think they could have won the quiet way—sooner and with vastly less cost to their own country.

But if you push Ol' Lyndon you are in trouble with an aroused poor Southern white who has accommodated to defeat by becoming a Northerner.

And it blinded him, fogged his mind, and the only message he got was the one already inside: we have the power to finish the job.

So at that juncture he was neither candid nor shrewd. He did not go back to the Congress, and he did not withdraw the American combat units.

He had blanked out what he had written to Kennedy in May, 1961. "At some point we may be faced with the further decision of whether we commit major United

States forces to the area or cut our losses and with-draw. . . . We must remain master in this decision."[26]

Only much later, after the white Northern liberal orthodoxy had run its course into horror, did Johnson's mind begin to clear. The public, first aroused by the students, began slowly to come awake and act as citizens with a will to "remain master in this decision." Then Têt. Lyndon goes on for pages about how the situation was stabilized, but most of it should be read as an uncon-scious record of the way he came to terms with the truth that it was all over.

So he went to the river.

He argues cogently that his push for the blacks and the poor had more than a bit to do with the last trip to Texas. Forcing the nation to confront the truth that the nobodies were somebodies did strengthen the right. It is a paradox appropriate to our ongoing moment of truth. The left moved us onto the road out of the war but the right retained the initiative at home.

To Robert Kennedy, Johnson was brave and honest.[27]

"I'm not that pure, but I am scared."

I see no point in belaboring Ol' Lyndon anymore.

The responsibility and the opportunities are now ours.

[26] *Pentagon Papers*, p. 130.

[27] Johnson, *The Vantage Point*, p. 541.

VI

Excelsior!

Almost everyone who has tried to make sense of Richard Milhous Nixon has acknowledged serious doubts about the value of the effort, admitted spells of boredom and outbursts of anger, and confessed recurrent frustration in finding and understanding the man. Their exasperation calls to mind the old children's game: "Nixon, Nixon, who's got *the* Nixon?"

The answer, very probably, is nobody. Not even Nixon.

If that is correct, and I think it is, then we can be clear about the reason for our unhappiness, anger, and fear. It is a shell game without any pea.

The support for this interpretation begins to emerge as one reviews other explanations of the man. One approach, offered by liberals and radicals (and some old-fashioned conservatives), pictures him as a bad or evil man embarked upon a brilliant and determined campaign to redefine traditional values in such narrow terms as to exclude most of us from consequential citizenship.[1] Without

---

[1] This view was first advanced during and after Nixon's initial campaign against Jerry Voorhis.

Nixon in the White House: The Frustration of Power by Rowland Evans, Jr., and Robert D. Novak (Random House).

The First Two Years of the Nixon Watch by John Osborne (Liveright).

denying the harmful effects, for example, of his slap-dash anticommunism, and recognizing that he does display malice and meanness, I think that interpretation breaks down for one basic reason: Nixon is neither that imaginative nor coherent. Being evil is a *heavy* trip.

A second analysis explains Nixon as first and always a politician. While admitting that he is guided by a few general values (such as capitalism and a distorted Protestant piety), and differing among themselves about his ability to deal with real issues and problems, these Nixonologists agree that he acts largely to obtain and retain public office. One gets the impression, for example, that Dwight David Eisenhower made that estimate of Nixon—giving him a B in shallowness and a D in leadership. A good bit of Nixon's career can be explained by this political analysis and his trips to China and Russia have revived its appeal after his earlier behavior as President had raised serious questions about its accuracy.

That approach has a major weakness, however, because defining a man as a politician does not—in and of itself—tell us how and why he responds to public moods and pressures (or to advice from confidants). It is not convincing to meet that objection by calling Nixon a pure politician (for whom office is all) who occasionally makes a mistake. Power is not his sole objective, and his gaffes do follow a pattern. The strongest statements of the political analysis have been offered by Ralph de Toledano and Garry Wills, who explain Nixon as the politician as self-made man.[2]

---

[2] R. de Toledano, *One Man Alone: Richard Nixon* (Funk and Wagnalls, 1969); G. Wills, *Nixon Agonistes: The Crisis of the Self-Made Man* (Signet, 1971).

Wills has attracted more attention because he offers an elaborate discussion of market place individualism and liberalism, because he digresses at great length on various current issues (Nixon disappears for pages on end), and because he is sympathetically critical instead of simply sympathetic. But one cannot read the books consecutively without becoming aware of their important similarities. Toledano's book (the earlier) is a hopper car full of data, and his interpretation is basically the same as the one offered by Wills. Taken together, they almost convince one that Nixon can be understood as the grade C self-made man as politician.

But only almost.

The first reservation arises from the information provided by Toledano and Wills that is not explained by their interpretation (give them high marks for that), from data supplied by Nixon himself,[3] and from further evidence offered in the collection of essays by John Osborne and the book by Rowland Evans and Robert D. Novak. The second weakness involves a central point in the theory of the self-made man. It is this: the classic self-made man does get made. He struggles upward until he makes the place that offers him the opportunity to fulfill himself. Then he proceeds to fulfill himself and, according to the theory, that personal fulfillment contributes to the general welfare.[4] Having earned success, the self-made

---

[3] As in, but by no means restricted to, R. M. Nixon, *Six Crises* (Doubleday, 1962). I have consulted an extensive range of materials beginning with the record of his first campaign.

[4] Such action, as we all now know, does not produce the general welfare. But that is a weakness in the broad Smithian theory of individualism/liberalism; and here the focus is on a specific person.

man is at peace.

And so the politician as self-made man explanation will not work for Nixon.

First, Nixon reveals no sense of the place where, *as himself*, he should stop and fulfill himself. It most probably was the House of Representatives; but, typically, he displayed so little recognition of place that he never became involved as a congressman (or even as a senator).[5]

Hence, second, there is nowhere any display of the self-made man's competence that becomes excellence in the proper place.

And so, third, there is no psychological ease and contentment.

We must therefore turn elsewhere for assistance in understanding Nixon. Specifically to the insight (first advanced by the Germans) about the middle-class individual who, denied any opportunity to realize himself as a consequential member of society (no sense of place or fulfillment), flees forward to escape destruction. To stop is to die because flight is identity. Life is a sequence of problems rather than a mix of difficulties, opportunities, and realization. And problems are solved either by fleeing past them or by resolving them into ever bigger problems.

Toledano, Evans and Novak, and Osborne supply much evidence for this analysis of Nixon, and Wills seems at one or two points about ready to slide into it without stating it. And Murray Kempton caught the essence without pausing to develop it: "The real Mr. Nixon just rushes

---

[5] Evans and Novak see this point, *Nixon in the White House*, p. 106; and it is very apparent in Nixon's various autobiographical ruminations.

past us in ill-concealed flight."[6] But the unnerving part of it all is that Nixon not only documents the interpretation in classic form but seems at times to perceive the truth and ask for help by supplying more evidence.

This is most apparent, perhaps, in *Six Crises*, though the pattern reappears in later interviews. Once the flight has begun, Nixon explains, a man "can never become adjusted to a more leisurely and orderly pace." "When you have won one battle is the time you should step up your effort to win another—until final victory is achieved."[7] But there can be no end because final victory is never defined. Nixon's bumbling effort in *Six Crises* to construct a psychological theory of crisis reads more like a public warning and a cry for help—watch me and grab me because I cannot stop myself. Father John Cronin, one of his earliest advisers, caught it all in one pithy sentence: "There is something in Nixon that will not let well enough alone." So did Toledano: "Nixon has always run scared."[8]

"Once you get into this great stream of history," Nixon screams at us as he races by, "you can't get out."[9] He was so anxious to avoid having to come ashore after he lost the race for governor in California that he was even willing to accept help from the Eastern Establishment, which he has always held responsible for blocking his way forward. "The main thing," he remarked about the job

---

[6]M. Kempton, *The New York Review of Books*, January 27, 1972, p. 21.

[7]Nixon, *Six Crises*, pp. 426, 38, 61.

[8]Wills, *Nixon Agonistes*, p. 38; Toledano, *One Man Alone*, p. 295.

[9]Toledano, *One Man Alone*, p. 193.

they offered, "it is a place where you can't slow down—a fast track. Any person tends to vegetate unless he is moving on a fast track."[10] But even the action in a major law firm at the center of the corporate power structure was not enough. He told one associate that he would die in four years if that was the end of the road.[11] As for a life of relaxation, pleasure, and contemplation—"nothing could be more pitiful."[12]

└ The politician as a man in flight is very largely limited to being the politician as campaigner. And that is Nixon's record. There is no sense of self to provide the basis for a philosophy (even an ideology), and neither time nor confidence to develop issues or answers. Hence the gross exaggerations and wild distortions about his opponents (Dean Acheson as an architect of "retreat and appeasement"); his manipulative and titillating secrecy about himself ("Is there a new Nixon? . . . You've got to answer the question yourself"); and his persistent evasion of issues by laying down a pepper-gas smoke screen of rhetoric about liberty, indivualism, and responsibility.[13] Osborne is correct: Nixon must "be faulted for a fundamental lack of political honor."[14]┘

There are many justifications for that judgment, but perhaps the most convincing one is Nixon's 1968 bargain

---

[10]Ibid., p. 332.

[11]Osborne, *Nixon Watch*, p. 136.

[12]Wills, *Nixon Agonistes*, p. 28.

[13]Nixon, *Six Crises*, p. 63; Osborne, *Nixon Watch*, pp. 4-5; Evans and Novak, *Nixon in the White House*, p. 367; and see Toledano's accounts of the various campaigns.

[14]Osborne, *Nixon Watch*, p. 6.

with the Southern extremists, which won him the en-
dorsement of Strom Thurmond. Even if John Quincy
Adams and Henry Clay actually did agree (in 1824) to
divvy up the White House and the Department of State,
their higgle-haggle was by comparison a child's game in
the sandbox. Nixon risked—*and very nearly lost*—the
chance for American society to continue functioning
while undertaking to transform itself into a community.
He could make a case for tucking himself into Strom
Thurmond's vest pocket if he had done so because he was
openly and honestly committed to white supremacy, or if
he had acted on a broader concern to bring rational and
responsible white Southerners back into the national community (and thereby create pressure on white Northerners
to mop up their own mess). But not Nixon. He was
merely prejudiced and, even more, desperate to avoid having to terminate his lifelong flight forward.

The most generous thing to say is that he had a secret
hope that being President would give him the identity he
had never been able to create. A frightening example of
the man who thinks the role makes the man. To be sure,
the Presidency *is* one of the two or three offices in world
politics (at least since 1860) that have the psychological
power to bring out the best in a man. But it cannot work
miracles. Nor is it a loom on which to weave finished
cloth from raw fiber.

Lest there be any misunderstanding, Nixon does contain some raw fiber. He does have considerable native
intelligence. He does have some sense of what is involved
in study and thought. (But he always talks more about
the setting than the process, and his intellectual strategy
of war-gaming a subject is the dead end of the problem-

life.) He has, under special conditions, ers. And he does have a fuzzy idealism honest concern for the poor and others w. stunted by the system.[15]

The le is that even all of that is not enough by half. There is simply no sense of self, no putting it together by Nixon. The most wrenching evidence lies in the stories about Pat trying to stop his flight. No doubt she is square, but she knows who she is and she wants a chance to realize her particular humanity. But Nixon broke his written promise to her to leave politics, confront himself, and thereby begin the struggle to fulfill himself—and her. Her anger is healthy.

Like ours.

And so into the White House. Where the private weakness becomes the public terror. Lack of identity compounded by incompetence compounded by little comprehension of American reality. "I've always thought this country could run itself domestically without a President."[16]

Incredible.

No purpose, no program, not even any pragmatics; no ability even to keep on his staff the men who offered leadership to counter his weakness; not even any idea of how to pay the debt to Strom Thurmond. Evans and Novak, and Osborne, tell this part of the story in considerable (and chilling) detail. After two terrifying efforts to destroy the integrity of the Supreme Court (which is

[15] Wills, *Nixon Agonistes*, p. 154; Evans and Novak, *Nixon in the White House*, p. 28; and see Osborne, "After Three Years," *New Republic*, January 15, 1972, pp. 14-15.

[16] Evans and Novak, *Nixon in the White House*, p. 11.

about the only established institution that blacks can believe in), Nixon blundered into a solution to that problem. Undertaking to use the Executive Department to weaken the law that the President is sworn to uphold, Nixon discovered that the law on school desegregation would have to be changed for Thurmond to have his way.[17]

So much for John Mitchell as a lawyer. But Nixon was off the hook, piously explaining to old Strom that he had no recourse but to enforce the law.

As a man who recognized what was going on, and what was at stake (if not what to do), Daniel Patrick Moynihan did his utmost to give Nixon some sense of identity. Appealing to the President's inherent conservatism and his vague idealism, he suggested that Nixon become America's Benjamin Disraeli. Find out who you are by aping a British prime minister who saw himself as the Tory as Reformer.[18]

Imaginative, and worth a try.

And it just might have worked if Nixon could have found the guts to fire (or ignore) Mitchell, and if the other Harvard professor in the White House had not countered by offering Nixon the image of a Woodrow Wilson reinforced and hardened with some realism from Prince Klemens von Metternich. Moynihan (and others who knew even more about America) hung on long enough to put together a reform package dealing with welfare, the draft, the tax system, social security, the

---

[17] Ibid., pp. 19, 24, 30, 49, 137ff., 409; Osborne, *Nixon Watch*, p. 45.

[18] Evans and Novak, *Nixon in the White House*, p. 212.

electoral process, foreign aid, and the environment.[19] But again, the politician as campaigner lacked the skill and dedication required to finesse and muscle the program through the Congress.

John Mitchell and Henry Kissinger knew their man. Mitchell blocked Nixon from any serious effort to become a latter-day Disraeli by deploying the force of his will and by keeping the campaign blinders tied on tight. Kissinger understood (or sensed) the more fundamental point: for a man fleeing forward, the last frontier is the world. There is the virgin land where a man can find and fulfill himself.[20] And, no doubt about it, the making of foreign policy within *that* idiom *is* the fastest track of all.

Having scrambled free of Thurmond, and been pulled away from Moynihan, Nixon joyously launched the ultimate crusade to realize the vision of St. Woodrow. Wilson was "our greatest President," Nixon explained, the man who "had the greatest vision of America's world role."[21] America must regenerate "a crusading zeal, not just to hold our own but to change the world—including the Communist world—and to win ... without a hot war." "You cannot win a battle in any arena of life merely by defending yourself."[22]

Eisenhower had no more use for that concept of global benevolent empire than he did for most of Nixon's other suggestions, but Dick could never learn the important things from Ike. The man fleeing forward is inherently

---

[19] Ibid., p. 241 for a good summary; but also see Osborne.

[20] Here see H. N. Smith, *Virgin Land* (Vintage, 1957).

[21] Wills, *Nixon Agonistes*, pp. 30-31.

[22] Nixon, *Six Crises*, pp. 68, 83.

unable to understand the man who com_
of the tortoise and the hare. So Nixon did
simply smoldered on the slow track provideu
Presidency. But the fires of world salvation le
ward when President John Fitzgerald Kennedy asx   .m
what to do after the defeat at the Bay of Pigs. Nixon told
Kennedy to "find a proper legal cover" and topple Castro
with the Marines.[23]

So much for Nixon as a lawyer.

Once again running free after 1960, Nixon revived his
natural rhetoric: the "sellout" of the "enslaved people in
Eastern Europe"; the necessity "to bring freedom to the
communist world"; and the crisis of America's "*confidence*" in its ability to realize such goals. He was con-
temptuous of the suggestion that there might be limits. "I
completely reject the idea that there are so-called peripheral areas, collateral areas—like Cuba and Vietnam—that
are not important."[24]

But the consequences of acting on that view of Vietnam could not be ignored by the politician as campaigner.
When Democrats began using the issue against Democrats,
Nixon had to hurry-scurry about for ways to sustain St.
Woodrow's crusade. His tactical response was to follow
Wilson's lead in distorting the principle of self-determination to mean self-determination for those who accepted
the American empire. Meaning Vietnamization maintained
with American aid and airpower. That offered the possibility of withdrawing American ground troops, which

---

[23]Toledano, *One Man Alone*, p. 315.

[24]Ibid., pp. 333-36, where he provides a good review of this
period, and in particular of the series of articles in *The Reader's
Digest*.

would help Nixon reach the White House—and also provide time to devise a new strategy capable of realizing the Wilsonian vision.)

Nixon might yet squeak through with that ploy in Vietnam in spite of its inherent weaknesses, and even though two typical actions almost ended his chance to develop a new strategy. Instead of making a full commitment to withdrawal, and then working out a rational plan that would leave no unprotected American supply troops (and at the same time offer a basis for serious negotiations in Paris), Nixon floundered into the dangerous necessity of having to mount a defensive offensive. That meant Cambodia.

He compounded that mistake because, always fleeing forward, he had never taken the time to understand the opposition to the war. He panicked in the face of the upheaval that was intensified by the killings at Kent State and Jackson State. Almost in a state of funk, the Administration was saved by the very kind of people that Nixon had damned throughout his public career, meaning the radicals who were committed to creating an American community, the liberals who were trying to reform the Establishment, and the conservatives who were trying to use their power responsibly. But, given the moment of grace, which he does not even yet comprehend, he stumbled up and forward toward the great vision.

"We are now in a position to give the world all the good things that Britain offered in her Empire without any of the disadvantages of nineteenth-century colonialism."[25] To the charge that such an approach still means

---

[25]Wills, *Nixon Agonistes*, p. 30.

NEO-WILSONIAN

empire, he offered this response: colonialism is not as bad
as communism.[26] All vintage Wilson. Including the unwillingness to acknowledge past mistakes and accom-
modate gracefully, and the determination "never [to]
settle for second best in anything."[27] Even including the
trips to China and Russia. He is Wilson, this time with an
assist from Metternich, going to Versailles. It involves the
same misunderstanding and mistaken judgment. Wilson
should have gone first to Leningrad, and Nixon should go
first to Hanoi.

Yet, whatever our deep reservations about Nixon, let
us give him full credit (whatever his motives) for renewing
the dialogue with China. To worry that issue is to miss
the vital point, which is that the relationship cannot be
developed creatively within the Wilsonian idiom. Wilson
saw opening the door to China as the way to Americanize
the Orient. Nixon still chases that fantasy. He is not only
"totally unwilling to cede US influence in any part of the
world where it exists," but is determined to extend it
wherever possible.[28] A man still worried about being No.
1 in a world where such competitiveness is the one attitude guaranteed to produce disaster deserves our sympathy and concern—but not our votes.

WRONG

The same judgment holds true for Nixon's negotiations
with the Russians. The trouble is that he sees himself as
structuring the world for a new Pax Americana that will
enable the United States to continue its misguided efforts

---

[26]Toledano, *One Man Alone*, p. 225.

[27]Evans and Novak, *Nixon in the White House*, p. 29; Nixon, *Six Crises*, pp. 454-55.

[28]Evans and Novak, *Nixon in the White House*, p. 79.

to ape the role that Great Britain played in the nineteenth century. The approach revealed an almost total lack of any sense of history that in turn leads on to outrageous terrifying actions in Vietnam, and to an irresponsible neglect of domestic affairs. It also places the fate of the world almost wholly in the hands of the Russians and the Chinese. That is an ironic, if also frightening, commentary on a man who for so long warned us about the irrationality of communism. Their prudence has so far saved us but it is time to change the outlook that forces others to accept so much of the responsibility for the peace of the world.

The most helpful thing we can do is to make sure that Dick honors his promise to Pat. This is the moment, Mr. President, to stop fleeing forward. Go home and explore the vast inner frontiers. The insight you had back in 1966 is the place to start. "I'd like to write two or three books a year, go to one of the fine schools—Oxford, for instance—just teach, read, and write."[29] Oxford may be a bit much, but the idea is sound.

Go ahead, turn Wilson on his head. Become an imperial politician devoted to scholarship. It offers the most promising way for you to help the rest of us realize the vision of a world of brotherhood and peace.

---

[29] As recounted in Osborne, *Nixon Watch*, p. 135.